LATIN GRILL

LATIN GRILL

Sultry and Simple Food for
Red-Hot Dinners and Parties

by RAFAEL PALOMINO with ARLEN GARGAGLIANO
Photographs by Dan Goldberg

CHRONICLE BOOKS
SAN FRANCISCO

Library of Congress Cataloging-in-Publication Data available.

ISBN 978-0-8118-6660-6

Manufactured in China

Designed and typeset by Design Army
Photographs by Dan Goldberg
Food Styling by Erin Quon
Food Styling Assistants: Alexa Hyman and Victoria Woollard
Prop Styling by Ethel Brennan
Digital Tech: Eduardo Navarro

THE PHOTOGRAPHER WOULD LIKE TO THANK ERIN QUON AND TATUM QUON
FOR SHARING THEIR HOME WITH US; IT PROVIDED A BEAUTIFUL
BACKDROP FOR THE PHOTOGRAPHS IN THIS BOOK.

10 9 8 7 6 5 4 3 2 1

Chronicle Books LLC
680 Second Street
San Francisco, California 94107
www.chroniclebooks.com

DEDICATED TO ALL WHO SHARE OUR LOVE OF FOOD, FAMILY, AND FRIENDS.

Acknowledgments

Thank you to my terrific writer, Arlen Gargagliano; my agent, Jane Dystel; my editor, Bill LeBlond, along with Sarah Billingsley; Doug Ogan, Anne Donnard, Ben Kasman, Peter Perez, and the staff at Chronicle Books; my Chronicle publicity manager, David Hawk; and my staff at Sonora, Pacífico, and Greenwich Tavern.

—Rafael Palomino

TABLE OF CONTENTS

HOLA

(hello)

The golden sunlight illuminates smiling faces as everyone enjoys appetizers of freshly toasted tortillas, topped with prosciutto and shaved Manchego cheese. Grown-ups enjoy mango sangría from wine glasses. The kids, meanwhile, are munching on grilled *arepas* (Colombian corncakes), in between playing soccer and sipping strawberry mango lemonade. Dinner, barbecued Chilean salmon brushed with soy *panela* (rich brown sugar) glaze, is just about ready, as is the side dish of Cartagena-style grilled pineapple rice, along with grilled portobello mushrooms topped with a fresh mint and pecan-studded pesto. It's late Sunday afternoon—the time when we all get to kick back with friends and family—and I'm exactly where I want to be: at home, grilling and relaxing!

Grilling is an intrinsic part of both my cultures. Every time I go back to my native Colombia, I can't wait to sink my teeth into an *Asado Bogotano*: a Bogotá-style barbecue that includes perfectly caramelized and fragrant corn on the cob, seared chorizo—classic Colombian sausage—and a roasted ripe plantain, which, upon peeling, will yield golden and perfectly sweet meat. The elements in this grilled dish vary somewhat throughout my home city, but one thing remains constant: the flavors of this and every barbecue—thanks to one of the world's oldest cooking methods—yield a depth of taste unmatched by any other type of cookery. Here at home in New York, I treat my family and friends to grilled dinners (inside and outside the restaurants!) just about every week.

This book presents you with a collection of recipes for easy-to-make grilled dishes, several cooling ceviches, and fabulous sides, including colorful and tasty salads, delicious desserts, and an assortment of festive drinks to complement them all. These dishes, inspired by my years in Colombia, my travels, my studies in France, and my personal and professional grilling experience, are especially designed to be tasty without being weighted down with too much toiling. Whether it's for a summertime barbecue or a midwinter get-together, this book offers a treasure chest of fun, gorgeous, tasty—and healthful—dishes to choose from. Here I'm using the terms *barbecue* and *grill* synonymously, though technically they're different; one refers to cooking on direct heat—grilling—while the other refers to cooking using indirect heat. But the bottom line for me is that we're talking about cooking over fire. The fire can come from charcoal, gas, or wood.

Latin Grill is for people who enjoy grilling and who enjoy extending the warmth of their homes to their families and friends. Following in the tradition of my other books—*Viva la Vida*, *Nueva Salsa*, and *Fiesta Latina*—the recipes in this collection are accessible, clear, and uncomplicated; you won't find overwhelming numbers of hard-to-find ingredients in these ingredient lists. But unlike *Fiesta Latina*, which is its predecessor, *Latin Grill* focuses on the barbecue, and its recipes are generally somewhat simpler.

Latin Grill presents all aspects of a barbecued dinner—including simple marinades, fruit-filled barbecue sauces (mango, pomegranate, coco, and citrus), appetizers, side dishes and dipping sauces, main dishes, desserts, and cocktails. Meals can start with appetizers like Yellowfin Tuna and Mango Vodka Ceviche—which is at once exotic yet elegant and festive. They can continue with a salad, like my simple and incredibly tasty Grilled Caesar Salad, and lead into my sirloin steak grilled medium-rare and lightly topped with Chipotle-Mango Barbecue Sauce. Or you could go with Grilled Lobster Tails with Paprika-Garlic Oil—like the kind you might enjoy in Lima, Peru—with a light brush of spark that leaves your mouth with a deliciously lingering aftertaste. Dinner could be followed by a captivating Semisweet Chocolate and Coffee Brioche Bread Pudding, served with dulce de leche ice cream or perhaps a dreamy coconut flan, drizzled with tropical guava sauce kisses. The point, my friends, is that potential combinations are both numerous and wonderful!

As in my other books, *Latin Grill* welcomes readers with recipes that are accurate, enticing, and delicious. Ingredients, as well as alternatives, are listed and explained in a comprehensive manner. Though the passion behind this book is similar to that found in my other works, *Latin Grill* focuses on my style of home entertaining, divulging recipes for dishes with a depth of flavor that family members *and* customers have grown to respect, adore, and crave.

My restaurants—Sonora in Port Chester, New York; Pacífico in both New Haven, Connecticut, and Lehigh, Pennsylvania; and Greenwich Tavern in Greenwich, Connecticut—feature my brand of Nuevo Latino, one that combines my Colombian heritage, my French—and New York City—restaurant education, and the knowledge I've harvested through years of being a chef, restaurateur, host, and father. Though my multiple kitchens are different from one another, my culinary philosophy remains constant: food should be fun to create, delicious to behold, and fabulous to consume.

THE BOTTOM LINE FOR ME IS THAT WE'RE TALKING ABOUT COOKING OVER FIRE.

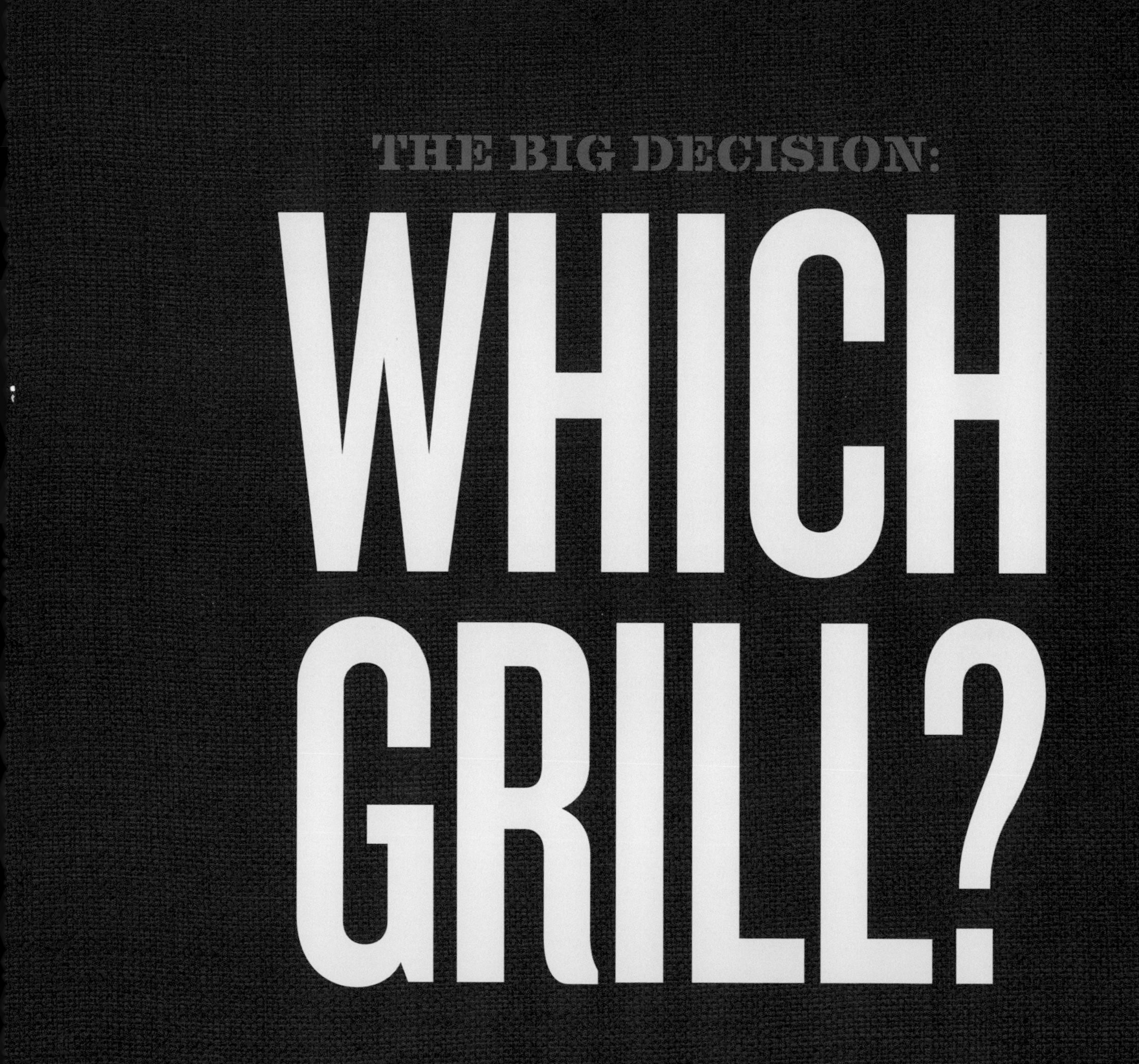
THE BIG DECISION:
WHICH
GRILL?

When it comes to grilling, the biggest choice as far as source of fire is charcoal versus gas. Ideally, if you have the space and inclination, you should have both! Here are a few of the features of each, as well as an explanation of my own home choice: the gas grill.

The beauty of the charcoal grill, aside from the flavor it imparts to the food cooked on it, is that it's portable—and easy to move. It's my first choice for picnicking and tailgating! (Though there are portable gas grills, too.) On the downside, especially for impatient cooks like me, it takes some time to get a charcoal grill ready: between twenty-five and thirty-five minutes. And then, while the flame can certainly be hot, it's not usually even. Charcoal grills also necessitate the building and maintaining of a fire and then the disposing of ashes; since I don't have an official—okay, paid—cleanup crew at home, keeping it neater and simpler is one of my home-cooking priorities!

So, why do I prefer gas grills? Basically, as I just mentioned, it's the simplicity and the convenience that have won me over. First, gas grills don't involve maintaining a live fire, they light quickly, and they can be ready for use in about fifteen minutes. Also, I enjoy the delivery of consistent heat—and the fact that I don't have to stop, as I've done with charcoal grilling, to "rebuild" a fire. Because of these two key features, my outdoor grilling season has been lengthened; I enjoy early spring and late fall (and occasional winter!) grilling. Yet another advantage of gas grills is that they generally have larger cooking surfaces—which is key if you're usually cooking for a crowd, or, as in my case, hungry teenagers! I'd suggest looking for a grill with at least two burners and ideally with three or more. (My home choice, by the way, is the Viking fifty-three-inch Ultra-Premium Stainless Steel Cart.)

Also, though many die-hard charcoal grillers will tell you their food's flavor is consistently better, I say that using wood chips (like mesquite and hickory)—and chunks—is a way that gas grillers can add that fabulous smoky flavor. Look, the important thing is that you find what's best for you, and, honestly, the one you are going to use is the best one! My rule for both kinds of grilling? Plan ahead; make sure you've got plenty of fuel on hand before you start. You don't want to chance getting caught without it in the middle of your fiesta!

Also, no matter which grill you're using, you want to make sure of these three key points:

1. The grill must be clean, but the bars have to have enough oil; you can brush it or rub it with a clean rag and vegetable oil (to prevent sticking).

2. Also, for my recipes, your flame should always be medium high.

3. Keep the grill top open so that you can keep a careful eye on what's happening!

TOOLS

FOR GRILLING EN CASA (at home)

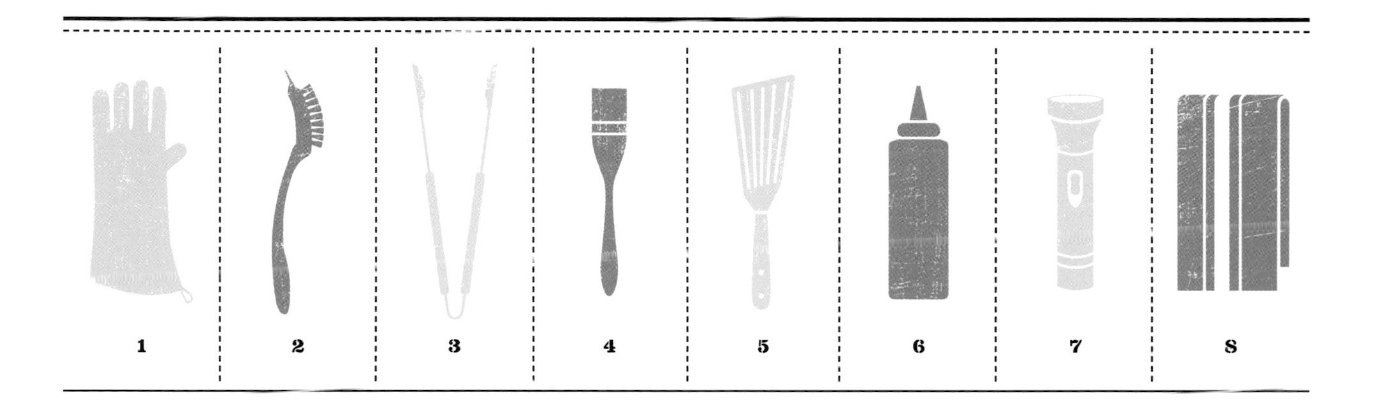

Whether I'm in the restaurant or at home, I've got all cooking toys ready! At home, I have my collection together (thanks in great part to my generous family and friends) and have listed my top grilling must-haves here:

1. **GLOVES:** It may sound obvious, but even I've been caught short at times. Long and fireproof are two rules to go by. After all, if you burn your hand, your wrist—or even your lower arm—you'll be pretty useless for the rest of the afternoon!

2. **GRILL BRUSH:** These brushes, ideally long handled for easier use, are essential for cleaning your grill and should be used each time you grill. I prefer brass to steel bristles because they're softer, they won't damage cooking grates—and they won't rust!

3. **TONGS:** I have quite an assortment of them. Primarily I think tongs are incredibly useful for both moving food around, and—if you're using charcoal—stirring the coals. (But these are not the same tong sets, mind you!) I recommend having at least one long set and one shorter set.

4. **BASTING BRUSHES:** These are great both to spread a bit of your marinade and to glaze your food with once the grill's done its work. I prefer the long-handled brushes designed for grilling.

5. **SPATULA:** A long "wide-footed" and flexible metal spatula—called a fish spatula—is ideal for flipping and turning your food on the grill.

Some other tools to keep on hand, and some points to keep in mind:

6. **A SQUIRT BOTTLE WITH WATER:** Keep this close by in case you get a rogue flame flare-up. (It's always better to be prepared.)

7. **PROPER LIGHTING:** Make sure you have an overhead light or a flashlight—you don't want to get stuck grilling in the dark.

8. **A KITCHEN TOWEL:** I never do anything without a towel nearby (but not close to the flame, of course!).

HOW TO USE THIS

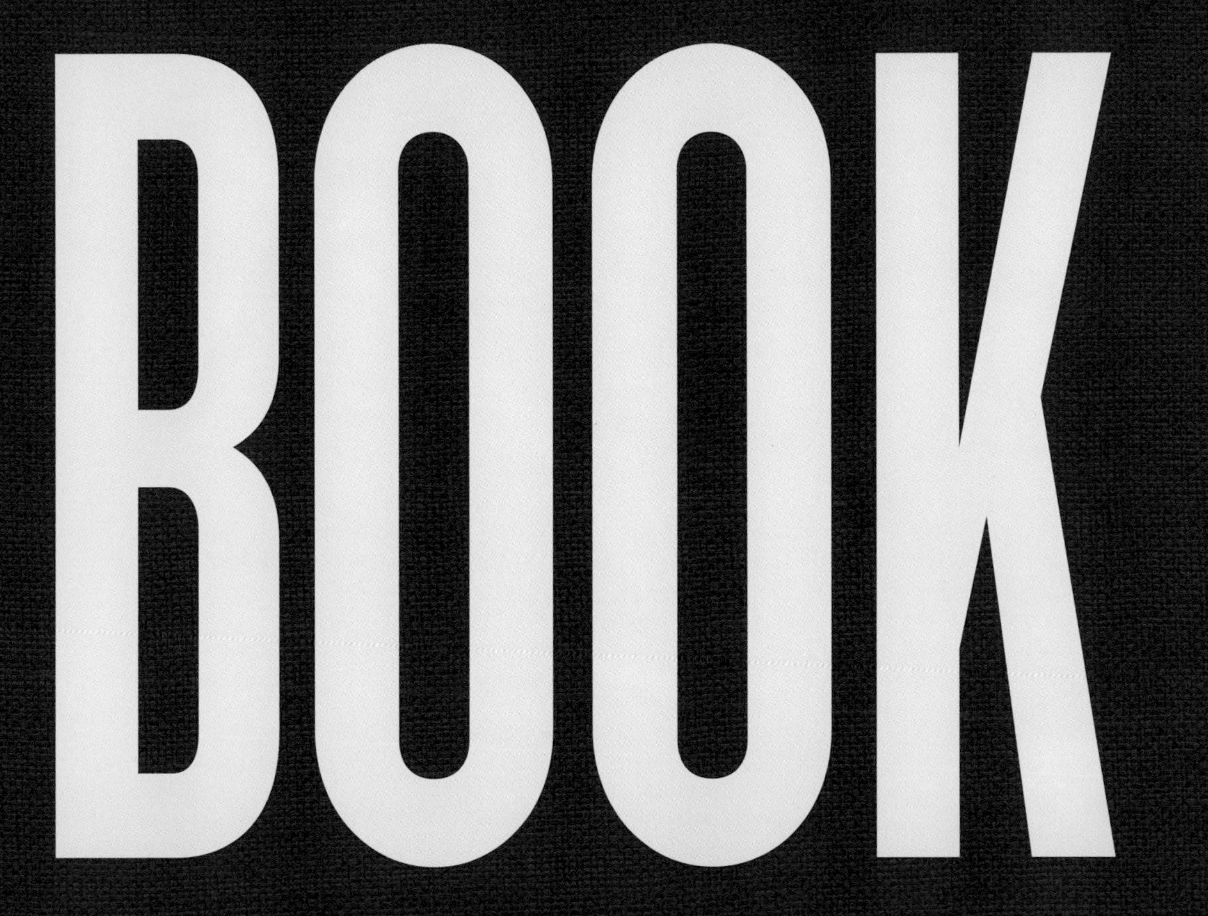

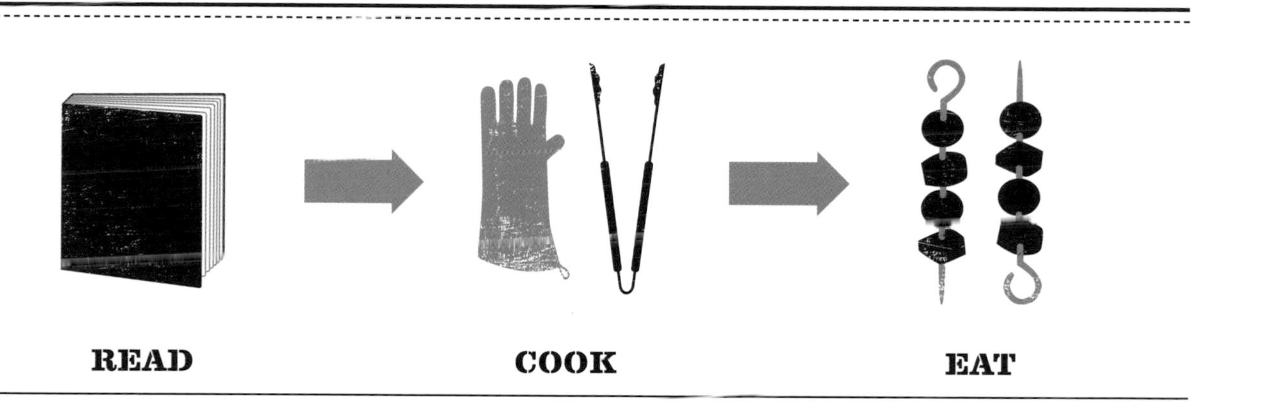

To start with, read through the book. Find dishes you'd like to explore; hopefully many will inspire you! Before you begin making these recipes for a big crowd, though, try them out on your friends and family. Then, when you're ready, branch out!

This book, like my others—and my restaurants—is designed to share flavors, dishes, and ingredients that I know and love. Anyone who knows me can tell you that the great passion I feel for food is one that I'm always interested in sharing with others. (Why else would I open five restaurants—AND entertain on the weekends?!) Since I can't meet all of you personally, please take this as an invitation—from me—to venture into new food territory, deepen the knowledge you have, or perhaps to try new interpretations of dishes.

The main idea, as always, is to have a great time! *¡Buen provecho!* Enjoy!

THE MAIN IDEA.

HAVE A GR

AS ALWAYS, IS TO

CEVICHES, TORTILLAS & AREPAS

{Chapter 1}

As a rule, we Latinos never offer drinks without *algo para picar*—something to snack on. This chapter shares my favorite appetizers, from sensual ceviches to crispy tortillas and savory corn cakes. Easy to prepare—and easier to devour—these treats are as perfect for a barbecue (or a brunch!) as they are for after-school or cocktail snacks. Have fun experimenting and mixing and matching. For example, you may want to try the corn cakes topped with my guacamole, or escabéche, one of my chimichurris. (Also try them alongside any of the meat dishes.)

The idea here is that you try different combinations of appetizers with different meals, and find your favorite balance of flavors. Of course, you also can do what I sometimes do at home: make a meal out of a wonderful assortment of them all!

OPPOSITE: *Yellowfin Tuna, Avocado, and Grilled Tomatillo Ceviche*

They're quick, they're first, they're . . .

SEA SCALLOPS, YELLOW TOMATOES, AND GRILLED ASPARAGUS CEVICHE

{ SERVINGS: 4 }

I remember becoming totally enamored with scallops. It happened in Nantucket, where I first enjoyed the freshest scallops I'd ever had. (Actually they were the smaller, and slightly sweeter, bay variety.) Since then, I've always managed to have scallops on my menus. Sea scallops, which have a mild, sweet, almost nutty flavor, are great to cook with because they can be combined with so many different vegetables. This very colorful ceviche is the perfect intro to any grilled dish.

6 asparagus spears
Vegetable oil
Kosher salt and freshly ground black pepper
4 sashimi-grade large sea scallops, each sliced into eighths
1 yellow (or red) beefsteak tomato, diced
Juice of **1** orange
Juice of **1** lime
½ red onion, minced
1 teaspoon balsamic vinegar

Light a fire in a charcoal or gas grill. Trim off the tough bottom of each asparagus spear by grasping each end and bending it gently until it snaps at its natural point of tenderness (usually ⅔ of the way down). If the spear has been trimmed, use a vegetable peeler and take off the outer skin of the bottom half of the remaining stalk.

Place the asparagus on a plate. Drizzle a bit of oil over the asparagus and turn the spears until they are lightly coated. Sprinkle with salt and pepper and turn again.

Grill the asparagus until the spears start to brown in spots, about 4 minutes total, turning halfway through. You want to keep it crisp and avoid overcooking it. As soon as it's cool enough to handle, slice, on an angle, into ¼-inch chunks. Set aside.

In a bowl, combine the scallops, tomato, and citrus juices. Add the onion, asparagus, and balsamic vinegar and mix well. Serve immediately.

STRIPED BASS AND GRILLED MUSHROOM CEVICHE

{ SERVINGS: 4 }

My autumn menu palette always includes an increase in mushrooms! But this ceviche has a bit of "let's hold on to summer" in the form of watermelon. I've also added a touch of spark in the form of a poblano pepper—but you can always make this more or less spicy depending on your own taste. Also, you can grill the mushrooms ahead of time, so that you can easily put the ceviche together just before your guests arrive. If you're looking to make this treat into a meal, you could serve it as a light lunch along with a green leafy salad.

1 pound sashimi-quality striped bass, skinned and diced into ¼-inch pieces
½ red onion, julienned
Juice of **4** oranges
Juice of **2** limes
Olive oil
4 shiitake mushrooms, cleaned and stemmed
4 wild domestic mushrooms, cleaned and stemmed
Kosher salt and freshly ground black pepper
2 tablespoons chopped cilantro leaves
½ poblano pepper, seeded, stemmed, and minced
16 watermelon balls (about 1½ cups)

In a large bowl, combine the striped bass with the onion and citrus juices. Let sit for about 10 minutes.

Light a fire in a charcoal or gas grill. Pour just a bit of oil on the mushrooms, season with salt and pepper, and place the mushrooms on the grill. Cook until they start to brown and soften, turning at least once, about 5 to 7 minutes all together. When cool enough to handle, cut into bite-size pieces.

Add the mushrooms, cilantro, and poblano to the bowl containing the bass, onion, and citrus juices. Stir in the melon balls and serve immediately.

YELLOWFIN TUNA AND MANGO VODKA CEVICHE

{ SERVINGS: 2 }

The combinations of flavors and colors in this ceviche remind me of the gorgeous colonial Colombian port city Cartagena. This recipe is the perfect starter for a barbecue because it's light, perfectly balanced, and very sexy (and, because of the vodka, for the twenty-one-and-over crowd). You can prep this ceviche ahead of time by assembling all the ingredients, and then, about 15 minutes prior to serving, add your tuna so that it "cooks" just a bit. The vodka infusion inspires those of the mango, citrus—and, of course, the luscious tuna. This cooling treat is ideal with a Pineapple and Raspberry White Sangría (page 130) on a sultry summer evening.

1 teaspoon honey
3 teaspoons soy sauce
Juice of **2** oranges
Juice of **2** limes
¼ cup finely diced red onion
¼ cup vodka
½ ripe mango, diced into ¼-inch cubes
1 tablespoon white balsamic vinegar
6 ounces sashimi-grade tuna, diced into ½-inch chunks
3 mint leaves, rolled and thinly cut (chiffonade*)
Kosher salt and freshly ground black pepper

In a medium bowl, whisk together the honey, soy sauce, and citrus juices. Stir in the onion, vodka, and mango. Add the vinegar and tuna. Stir in the mint leaves. Season with salt and pepper. Cover and refrigerate for no more than 15 minutes (you don't want the tuna to cook too much!) and serve immediately.

*CHIFFONADE is a French term that means "made of rags." To cut leaves in this way, stack them, roll them tightly, and cut them across with a sharp knife, which will produce fine ribbons.

YELLOWFIN TUNA, AVOCADO, AND GRILLED TOMATILLO CEVICHE

{ SERVINGS: 4 }

I learned about tomatillos when I went to the Las Lomas area of Mexico City to see Juanita, the mother of my best friend, Alberto. Today many of my Mexican-born restaurant employees incorporate this pre-Colombian husk tomato in many of their sauces—just as their ancestors have done for centuries. Tomatillos have many redeeming qualities in addition to being very healthful: they improve flavor, soften the kick of some hot chiles, and also enhance appetites! I like combining the smoky taste of the grilled tomatillos with the clean flavor of fresh tuna—as in this ceviche. As long as you prep the tomatillos ahead of time, you can put this ceviche together in just a few minutes—and it's a great starter before grilled meat entrées, like Grilled Skirt Steak with Basil-Garlic Olive Oil (page 82) or the Grilled Palomino Burger with Manchego Cheese and Avocado (page 85).

*TOMATILLOS can be found in larger supermarkets and in Latin markets. Remove their papery husks before grilling and rinse the fruit to remove the sticky coating.

3 small tomatillos*
2 tablespoons olive oil
½ cup balsamic vinegar
1 clove roasted garlic (see page 151)
½ cup fresh orange juice
¼ small red onion, diced
1 cup diced sashimi-grade tuna
2 small California avocados, diced
Kosher salt and freshly ground black pepper

Light a fire in a charcoal or gas grill. Cut the tomatillos into wedges and lightly oil them. Quickly grill the tomatillos so they're crisp-tender, a couple of minutes per side. Remove them from the grill and let cool slightly. Combine them with oil, vinegar, and garlic in a blender, and process until puréed. (You can do this up to 3 days ahead of time.)

At least 15 minutes prior to serving your ceviche, combine the orange juice, onion, and tuna in a medium bowl. Pour in the tomatillo purée and stir until blended. Add the diced avocado and gently toss. Season with salt and pepper. Let sit, covered and refrigerated, for 15 minutes, and then serve in chilled martini glasses.

TUNA TORO TIRADITO WITH GINGER SOY SAUCE

{ SERVINGS: 4 }

Just thinking about this Peruvian-style sashimi makes me crave it! It's fresh, clean, light—and very simple. In the restaurants, I serve this as an appetizer atop baby watercress; at home you can use that or your favorite mix of baby greens.

12 ounces sashimi-grade tuna, thinly sliced
1½ teaspoons grated fresh ginger
2 tablespoons soy sauce
1 tablespoon rice vinegar
2 tablespoons water
½ cup fresh-squeezed orange juice
Baby watercress for serving (about ¼ cup)

Chill four salad plates by placing them in the refrigerator for about half an hour prior to serving.

Place about 3 ounces of tuna in between two pieces of plastic wrap. Using a kitchen mallet, pound to spread. (You want the tuna to have a carpaccio-like thinness.) Repeat with the remaining tuna. Cover and place in the refrigerator until ready to serve.

In a small bowl, whisk together the ginger, soy sauce, rice vinegar, water, and orange juice. Plate the tuna and lightly top with the ginger soy sauce. Garnish each plate with about 1½ teaspoons of baby watercress and serve.

“JUST THINKING ABOUT THIS . . .
MAKES ME CRAVE IT!”

Flat and Fabulous

GRILLED FLOUR TORTILLAS

with Goat Cheese, Peruvian Olives, and Roasted Red and Yellow Peppers

{ SERVINGS: 4 }

When we opened Palomino in Greenwich, I gave myself the welcome challenge of infusing even more of my Mediterranean studies and experiences into my Latin-style cooking. The tasty results have been greeted with accolades by all! One of my new "techniques" is related to serving; it's this one—along with these flavors—that I'm sharing with you here. I started cutting my circle-shaped tortillas into squares and then folding them into triangles. (I fry the remaining dough and use the "chips" in my soup, but you can also sprinkle them on your salad.) This tortilla treat is perfect on its own as an appetizer, or as a lunch, as we've served in Palomino, along with a small salad.

4 burrito-size (10- or 12-inch) flour tortillas, trimmed into squares
4 tablespoons (one for each tortilla) crumbled goat cheese
4 tablespoons (one for each tortilla) roasted red and yellow peppers (see page 150)
1 small bunch baby arugula
2 tablespoons Peruvian Olive, Cilantro, and Thyme Tapenade (page 150)

Light a fire in a charcoal or gas grill. Set up your square tortillas on a clean work surface. Spread one tablespoon of the crumbled goat cheese on each tortilla. Spread a layer of the roasted peppers on top. Place, open faced, on the grill until the grill lines appear on the bottom, just about 1 minute. Add enough baby arugula to make a layer on top and top that with a dollop (1½ teaspoons) of tapenade on each tortilla. Fold into a triangle, cut into two smaller triangles, plate, and serve immediately.

TORTILLAS
with Palomino's Guacamole

{ MAKES ABOUT 2½ CUPS }

Even before I was asked to be a spokesperson for the Avocado Association in 2003, I was in love with this prehistoric-skinned fruit! Also called alligator pears, avocados offer a great nutty flavor to salsas, ceviches, salads—and to the dish that shows them off best: guacamole. I like to serve this guacamole with fresh (or grilled!) whole-wheat tortillas. I cut the tortillas into triangles so that guests can easily spread the guacamole on them and then fold the tortillas into small diagonal pockets. Or you can cut up your favorite corn tortillas and fry them until perfectly crisp—about 45 seconds in a deep fryer (at 450°F). Serve before any grilled entrée—or as a great snack with cocktails—like a Grilled Pineapple Mojito (page 133).

4 ripe California avocados, pitted, peeled, and coarsely chopped
Juice of **½** lime
1 medium red onion, diced
2 red beefsteak tomatoes, finely diced
1 teaspoon Tabasco (or according to taste)
1 teaspoon kosher salt
¼ cup chopped cilantro leaves
Whole-wheat tortillas (or your favorite flour tortillas), cut into triangles

In a large glass or ceramic bowl, combine the avocados and the lime juice. Use a fork to mash the two together (you can still have chunks, but it should be smooth for the most part). Stir in the onion, tomatoes, Tabasco, salt, and cilantro. Mix well. Spread immediately on your favorite tortillas or cover tightly and refrigerate for up to 1 day.

CRISP TORTILLA TOPPED WITH PROSCIUTTO

and Shaved Manchego Cheese

{ SERVINGS: 4 }

Not only is this appetizer supersimple, it's also great for kids. The combination of prosciutto and Manchego cheese works beautifully in this appetizer, which can easily be prepped ahead of time and grilled at the last minute. In addition to being a pre-dinner starter, this panini-like tortilla dish could be served as a lunch or a light dinner, with a big leafy green salad.

4 burrito-size (10- or 12-inch) tortillas
¾ cup shaved Manchego or aged Parmesan cheese
20 thin slices (or 8 whole slices) excellent-quality prosciutto
Baby arugula
Olive oil

Light a fire in a charcoal or gas grill. Place the tortillas on a clean work surface. Blanket each one with the shaved cheese and a layer of prosciutto. Fold the tortilla in half and grill, turning once, until the cheese softens, about 2 minutes total. Cut the tortillas into thirds (so you have 12 pieces total). Top with baby arugula and a splash of olive oil and serve.

GRILLED AREPAS

with Farmer's Cheese (or Queso Blanco)

{ SERVINGS: 4 }

It's not only nostalgia that makes me love *arepas*; it's also their versatility! These corncakes are hugely popular in many forms in my native Colombia and neighboring Venezuela (among other places) and have now actually caught on in many parts of the United States. What makes them especially wonderful is that they offer cooks fabulous flexibility as far as preparation. So here I'm giving you my basic recipe—and a serving suggestion—but please know you can add whatever you'd like (grilled corn, diced peppers, different cheeses, just to name a few possibilities).

Here I'm suggesting that you smear a bit of farmer's cheese—or Mexican *queso blanco*—on top. Great as an appetizer, these *arepas* are perfect with any cocktail!

1 cup corn kernels, fresh or frozen and thawed
¾ cup heated chicken stock (see page 144) or water
1 cup instant cornmeal
1½ teaspoons sugar
1 teaspoon sour cream
1 ounce Manchego cheese, grated
1 tablespoon butter, melted
½ cup farmer's cheese or Mexican *queso blanco*

In a blender, process the corn kernels and chicken stock until smooth. Pour the cornmeal into a large bowl. Stir in the sugar and sour cream. Pour in the chicken stock and corn mixture while stirring with your hands or a wooden spoon. Add the grated cheese. Form mixture into a ball. Then separate into 8 pieces. Roll each piece into a ball and then flatten into a pancake about ¼-inch thick and 2 inches in diameter (but rub your fingers around the edge so that it maintains its thickness). At this point you can cover the *arepas* with a damp kitchen towel and refrigerate them for up to 1 day before grilling.

Light a fire in a charcoal or gas grill. Brush the *arepas* lightly with the melted butter (for flavor and to prevent sticking). Grill the *arepas* until golden, about 3 minutes on each side. They should be toasted on the outside, but soft in the middle. Let cool to room temperature. Before serving, top with a spread of the farmer's cheese.

GRILLED SOFT-SHELL CRAB SANDWICH

with Avocado and Chipotle Tartar Sauce

{ SERVINGS: 4 }

During my last New Orleans visit, I became re-enamored with po' boys—especially when they are served up on my favorite Louisiana French bread. I love the simplicity of this sandwich; essentially it's a soft-shell crab cushioned between two pieces of tasty bread, topped with lettuce, tomato, and a touch of smoky chipotle tartar sauce and silky avocado. Though I still love the crawfish version, this one is a bit lighter. It goes beautifully with Mango Lemonade (page 128) or—one of my favorites—an ice-cold Negra Modelo.

4 soft-shell crabs
Kosher salt and freshly ground black pepper
4 brioche buns or potato bread rolls
2 teaspoons Chipotle Tartar Sauce (page 145)
4 leaves romaine lettuce
4 slices tomato
1 Hass avocado, pitted, peeled, and sliced

Light a fire in a charcoal or gas grill. Sprinkle the crabs with salt and pepper. Grill until the shells turn reddish, about 13 minutes on each side.

Meanwhile, place the rolls on a clean work surface and open them. Lightly coat one side of each with about ½ teaspoon of the tartar sauce. Then, to the uncoated sides, distribute the lettuce, tomato, and avocado slices. Top with the grilled crab. Close the sandwich, slice, and serve immediately.

“

I LOVE THE SIMPLICITY OF THIS SANDWICH.

”

SALADS & SIDES

(ENSALADAS Y ACOMPAÑAMIENTOS)

{Chapter 2}

Salads and side dishes can be as important as the stars of any meal. They should be simple—yet elegant enough to hold their own, especially because they often serve as introductions to the meal. Salads should be clean; their flavors—whether in layers or not—should be discernable. Salads like the *Hombre Pobre*—Poor Man's Salad—which infuses Italian ingredients in the form of the white balsamic vinaigrette, along with our local bread, Hudson Valley tomatoes, and basil, are an example of my ideal taste, content, and color balance. Also, don't be afraid to create new combinations by taking elements of one salad—like the sweet corn vinaigrette—and combining it with a different mixture of greens. The idea here is that you get inspired to try putting flavors together that you previously haven't tried! Here are some of my favorite barbecue salads and sides, along with additional suggestions and tips.

OPPOSITE: *Grilled Shrimp with Watercress and Sweet Corn Vinaigrette*

Simple, Colorful, and Tasty

(ENSALADAS)

HOMBRE POBRE

(Poor Man's Salad)

{ SERVINGS: 4 }

Whenever my writer, Arlen, has a barbecue—which is just about every Sunday in the summer—she makes this salad, which she believes has Italian roots (at least in her family!). It makes great use of leftover bread, as well as fresh tomatoes and basil, and it's not only simple, fresh, and tasty, it's also very flexible. You can vary dressing according to your taste (my Sweet Shallot Vinaigrette—on page 153—would also work well), or add different ingredients such as cucumber, mesclun lettuce, daikon radish—even potatoes. Serve this salad with any of the grilled dishes in the book.

1 garlic clove, minced
Kosher salt and freshly ground black pepper
2 tablespoons white balsamic vinegar
¼ cup olive oil
3 cups ½-inch cubes of crusty bread (preferably ciabatta)
1 pound fresh mozzarella, cut into ¼-inch chunks
1 pound vine-ripened red tomatoes, cut into ½-inch chunks
1 pound vine-ripened yellow tomatoes, cut into ½-inch chunks
½ cup fresh basil leaves, finely chopped

In a bowl, mash the garlic to a paste, using a pestle or the back of a spoon, along with a pinch of salt and pepper. Add the vinegar and whisk in the oil until blended.

In a medium bowl, combine the bread, mozzarella, tomatoes, and basil. Pour the oil and vinegar mixture on top and stir to coat. Let the salad stand at room temperature for about 15 minutes to allow the bread to soak up the dressing before serving.

GRILLED CAESAR SALAD

{ SERVINGS: 4 }

As I've mentioned before, my family is made up of total grill fans! One inspired summer afternoon, I decided I wanted to play with some additional ingredients on my grill; that's when I came up with this salad. It was an immediate hit! I like this salad because it goes well with every grilled main dish I've included in this book. And—if you're anything like my wife in your love of salads—you might just want to have this on its own!

1 head romaine lettuce, leaves rinsed and dried, tops and bottoms removed
Olive oil
⅓ cup shaved or grated Parmesan cheese
1 pinch kosher salt
2 teaspoons white balsamic vinegar
½ medium ripe avocado, sliced into quarters (Note: If it's too ripe, it won't hold up to grilling.)

Light a fire in a charcoal or gas grill. Separate the romaine lettuce leaves and place in a bowl. Brush just a bit of oil on the leaves, to lightly coat them for the grill.

Grill the lettuce just until grill marks are visible, about 1 minute, turning once. Cut the lettuce into bite-size chunks and place in a bowl. Add the Parmesan cheese, salt, and vinegar and toss. Add the avocado. Serve immediately.

GRILLED CALAMARI, TOMATO, CUCUMBER, AND ARUGULA SALAD

with Feta Cheese

{ SERVINGS: 4 }

This salad is certainly Greek influenced (and this goes beyond the feta cheese!). The combination of the strong and salty feta works so well with the slightly bitter arugula—and together they balance superbly with the sweet grilled calamari (which is velvety perfect when it's cooked right), cherry tomatoes, and crunchy cucumber. Because of the robust flavors of this salad, I like to serve it on its own, with a light cocktail, like my Mango Sangría (page 131).

1 pound tubes calamari, cleaned
Vegetable oil
1 pinch fresh minced garlic
1 pinch cumin
1 pinch paprika
Kosher salt and freshly ground black pepper
2 lemon wedges
2 bunches baby arugula, washed
8 cherry tomatoes, halved
½ seedless Japanese cucumber, with skin, sliced thinly
2 tablespoons olive oil
4 tablespoons crumbled feta cheese

Light a fire in a charcoal or gas grill.

Place the calamari tubes in a bowl and add a squirt of vegetable oil, the garlic, cumin, and paprika and season with salt and pepper. Squeeze the juice from 1 lemon wedge on top and mix well. Let sit for 15 minutes. Grill the calamari tubes just until they turn opaque, about 10 minutes. As soon as they're cool enough to handle, cut them into ¾-inch-thick rings. Set aside.

In a large bowl, combine the arugula with the tomatoes and cucumber slices. Mix well. Top with the grilled calamari, olive oil, the juice from the remaining lemon wedge, and the feta cheese. Toss to combine. Season with salt and pepper. Serve immediately.

GRILLED SHRIMP WITH WATERCRESS

and Sweet Corn Vinaigrette

{ SERVINGS: 6 }

The slight bitterness of watercress offers a perfect backdrop for the flavors of the grilled shrimp and sweet corn vinaigrette; the fresh apple and avocado add extra flavor and texture contrasts. You can prepare the vinaigrette a day before and then simply add the shrimp, apple, and avocado to the watercress bed. This salad is certainly a light meal on its own but can also be served with grilled fish, meat, or chicken.

1⅛ cups vegetable oil
3 ears corn, shucked and stemmed
Kosher salt and freshly ground black pepper
18 medium-size shrimp, peeled, cleaned, and deveined
1 pinch cumin
1 pinch paprika
1 shallot
½ cup white balsamic vinegar
1 large bunch watercress, tougher bottom stems removed
½ Hass avocado, pitted, peeled, and cut into ½-inch chunks
1 Granny Smith apple, peeled, cored, and sliced into ¼-inch-thick segments

Light a fire in a charcoal or gas grill. Squirt just a splash of oil atop the ears of corn and rub to spread. Sprinkle with salt and pepper. Place the corn on the grill and cook, rotating as needed, until lightly caramelized, about 10 minutes. Set the ears aside until they're cool enough to handle and then remove the kernels from the cob. Place the kernels into a bowl.

Meanwhile, in a large bowl, combine the shrimp with the cumin and paprika. Add a splash of oil and toss to coat. Grill until pink, turning once and making sure not to overcook (or they'll go from tender to rubbery!), between 6 and 8 minutes. Set aside.

In a blender, combine the corn kernels, shallot, 1 cup of vegetable oil, and the vinegar and process until blended (the vinaigrette should still have some texture).

Place the watercress in a large bowl. Top with the avocado and apple. Pour about ½ cup of the vinaigrette on top and gently toss. Transfer the watercress mixture to a platter for serving and top with the grilled shrimp. Serve immediately.

GRILLED SEA SCALLOPS WITH AVOCADO AND APPLE SALAD

{ **SERVINGS: 4** }

This light and clean salad brings me back to a visit I made many years ago to Mark Miller's Coyote Café. Mark's sense of balancing his dishes by using a diversity of fresh flavors—and his creations of great, simple food—inspire me to this day. Crisp and somewhat tart Granny Smith apples offer a perfect counterpoint to the buttery avocado and scallops. Enjoy this salad for lunch with grilled *arepas* (page 37) that you can top with my guacamole (page 34).

12 large sea scallops, side muscles trimmed, halved horizontally
Garlic Oil (page 151)
Kosher salt and freshly ground black pepper
1 avocado, pitted, peeled, and diced into bite-size chunks
1 Granny Smith apple, seeded and sliced into segments
1 yellow (or red beefsteak) tomato, seeded and diced
8 red grape tomatoes, halved
2 large handfuls baby arugula
Mustard Vinaigrette (page 149), according to taste

Thread the scallops onto 4 metal skewers (3 to a skewer) and coat the scallops lightly with Garlic Oil. Sprinkle with salt and pepper.

Light a fire in a charcoal or gas grill. Grill until the scallops are just opaque in the center, occasionally brushing with more Garlic Oil, about 3 minutes per side. Set aside.

In a large bowl, combine the diced avocado, apple, tomatoes, and baby arugula. Add the Mustard Vinaigrette and toss lightly. Serve immediately on either a platter or individual plates, topped with the grilled scallops.

PAN-SEARED DUCK BREAST AND PEAR ARUGULA GORGONZOLA SALAD

{ **SERVINGS: 4** }

The contrast of flavors in this salad is amazing: you've got the sweetness of the pears, the sharpness of the cheese, the light bitterness of the arugula, and the buttery duck—all bound together with a supportive and light vinaigrette! In my Greenwich restaurant, we typically caramelize the pears for this salad. (Heat a small saucepan with ½ cup water and ¼ cup raw sugar until dissolved and cook the pears until the water dissolves.) Because Bosc pears have flesh that is firmer and denser than other pear varieties, they're ideal for caramelizing—but they are also excellent for fresh eating, particularly by those who prefer a crisper texture. This could certainly be a meal by itself, or it could be served alongside Boiled Yuca with Cilantro Garlic Mojo (page 66), or with Grilled Pineapple Coconut Rice (page 67).

4 duck breast halves, boned
Kosher salt and freshly ground black pepper
2 handfuls baby arugula leaves
½ cup crumbled gorgonzola cheese
2 Bosc pears, diced into ½-inch chunks, caramelized (see headnote) or raw
Sweet Shallot Vinaigrette (page 153)

Place the duck breasts on a clean work surface. Trim off any excess fat and skin around the breast. There should be just enough skin to cover the breast. Shave off any additional skin or sinew on the surface of the meat. Using a very sharp knife and being careful to avoid cutting into the meat, score the skin of the duck breasts in a crisscross pattern. (This allows the fat to render during cooking, which will result in crispier skin.) Season both sides with salt and pepper.

Place a large sauté pan over high heat until very hot. Sear the breasts until some of the fat has melted and the skin is brown and crisp, about 7 minutes. Pour off the fat and discard. Turn and continue cooking for 5 or so minutes, or until the duck breast is still pink in the center. Let rest for about 5 minutes before slicing, on an angle, into ¼-inch-thick slices.

Spread the arugula leaves on a platter. Top with the gorgonzola and pears. Add the sliced duck and drizzle with the shallot vinaigrette just before serving.

GRILLED LAMB WITH GORGONZOLA AND GOAT CHEESE AND FRISÉE LETTUCE

{ **SERVINGS: 4** }

Though I created this dish for my restaurants on the East Coast, it was inspired by a West Coast visit I made—years ago—to Alice Waters's Chez Panisse in Berkeley, California. I was immediately smitten by her ability to combine fresh and excellent quality ingredients. As is the case of many chefs of my generation, I was permanently and positively impressed by the philosophy that she follows to this day: shop locally and eat organically. Her meals, characterized by simple and clean flavors, continue to be a driving force behind many of my creations. This salad is perfect when you're craving an all-in-one-style dinner. Besides, you can make it ahead of time and then sit down with your guests—along with a great bottle of Chilean wine, like Le Dix de Los Vascos, and fresh bread—and enjoy the whole meal together (instead of hopping up and down to grill!).

2 pounds boneless leg of lamb, silver skin removed, and cut into 1-inch chunks
1 teaspoon cumin
1 teaspoon paprika
Kosher salt and freshly ground black pepper
1 cup vegetable oil
½ cup white balsamic vinegar
Juice of **1** lime
8 ounces frisée lettuce
2 tablespoons grated goat cheese
2 ounces crumbled gorgonzola cheese
½ red beefsteak tomato, diced
1 ripe avocado, peeled, pitted, and diced into chunks
1 tablespoon Sweet Shallot Vinaigrette (page 153)

In a large bowl, combine the lamb chunks, cumin, and paprika. Season with salt and pepper and mix well. Stir in the oil, vinegar, and lime juice and mix to coat well. Cover and refrigerate for about 10 minutes.

Light a fire in a charcoal or gas grill. Grill the lamb, turning as needed, until medium-rare, about 7 minutes.

Meanwhile, combine the frisée lettuce, cheeses, tomato, and avocado on a platter. Add the vinaigrette and toss lightly. As soon as the lamb is cooked, slice the chunks and distribute them over the lettuce. Serve immediately.

Real men eat their greens, yellows, and reds

(ACOMPAÑAMIENTOS)

GRILLED ASPARAGUS SPEARS
with Wisconsin Blue Cheese Vinaigrette

{ SERVINGS: 4 }

I learned to respect blue cheese many moons ago, when I worked with Larry Forgione at An American Place. It was there that the robust, tangy, and sharp-flavored cheese appeared in so many dishes! I learned that it can be balanced beautifully by many softer flavors, as it is in this grilled asparagus salad. The salad can be served as a side dish at your barbecue or even as a lunch or light dinner; simply serve it atop a bed of fresh lettuce. Prepare the vinaigrette ahead of time so that you can just grill, top, and serve.

½ cup crumbled Wisconsin blue cheese (or your favorite), plus more as desired
¼ cup canola oil, plus additional for grilling
½ cup white balsamic vinegar
½ shallot, minced
4 basil leaves, rolled and thinly sliced (chiffonade, see page 26)
1 bunch asparagus
Kosher salt and freshly ground black pepper
Frisée lettuce for serving (optional)

Combine the blue cheese, the ¼ cup canola oil, the vinegar, and shallot and whisk. (You could even do this in a blender, but I like keeping some of the blue cheese chunks whole.) Stir in the basil. Set aside, or cover and refrigerate for up to 2 days before using.

Light a fire in a charcoal or gas grill. Trim off the tough bottom of each asparagus spear by grasping each end and bending it gently until it snaps at its natural point of tenderness (usually ⅔ of the way down). If the spear has been trimmed, use a vegetable peeler and take off the outer skin of the bottom half of the remaining stalk.

Place the asparagus on a plate. Drizzle a bit of oil over the asparagus and turn the spears until they are lightly coated. Sprinkle with salt and pepper and turn again.

Grill the asparagus until the spears start to brown in spots, about 4 minutes total, turning halfway through. You want to keep the asparagus crisp and avoid overcooking it.

Remove the asparagus from the heat and place atop a bed of frisée lettuce (if desired). Drizzle the blue cheese vinaigrette on top and serve.

GRILLED ASPARAGUS, SHIITAKE MUSHROOM AND ROASTED PEPPER ESCABECHE

{ SERVINGS: 4 }

The first time I enjoyed an escabéche, it was a Spanish-style traditional version of this fried and pickled fish dish. I was inspired to create a vegetarian version so my non-fish-eating customers could enjoy similar flavors. This simple—and tasty—plate is perfect as a side dish, served next to or on top of crusty bread, with a leafy green salad, or as a salsa served atop grilled fish or meat.

1 bunch asparagus spears
½ cup olive oil
Kosher salt and freshly ground black pepper
1 cup cleaned, stemmed, and diced shiitake mushrooms
2 tablespoons minced red onion
¼ cup white balsamic vinegar
½ cup roasted red (or yellow—or both!) peppers (see page 150), julienned

Light a fire in a charcoal or gas grill. Trim off the tough bottom of the asparagus spear by grasping each end and bending it gently until it snaps at its natural point of tenderness (usually ⅔ of the way down). If the spear has been trimmed, use a vegetable peeler and take off the outer skin of the bottom half of the remaining stalk.

Place the asparagus on a plate. Drizzle a bit of oil (from the ½ cup) over the asparagus and turn the spears until they are lightly coated. Sprinkle with salt and pepper and turn again.

Grill the asparagus until the spears start to brown in spots, about 4 minutes total, turning halfway through. You want to keep the asparagus crisp and avoid overcooking it. When they're cool enough to handle, slice the asparagus spears into ½-inch chunks.

Combine the asparagus with the remaining oil, the mushrooms, onion, vinegar, and roasted peppers. Let sit for about 5 minutes (or up to a few hours—without the asparagus) and serve.

YELLOW TOMATOES

Stuffed with Grilled Wild Mushrooms and Parmesan Cheese

{ SERVINGS: 4 }

This beautiful side dish is perfect not only because it looks gorgeous but also because it's totally consumable! This creation was inspired by a dish I had in Puerto Rico, where I enjoyed a typical *mofongo* (mashed plantain dish) served in a *pilón*—which is a kind of mortar. I thought then, "Wouldn't this be great in a tomato?" Since then, I've been dreaming up all kinds of tomato stuffers! My first choice—as far as mushroom fillers—is domestic oyster, shiitake, or portobellos, which you can easily grill (or sauté!) ahead of time. Also, Manchego is another delicious option for the cheese.

1 cup sliced oyster, shiitake, or portobello mushrooms (domestic or imported)
2 tablespoons olive oil
1 tablespoon minced shallots
¼ teaspoon chopped fresh rosemary
¼ teaspoon chopped fresh thyme
4 perfectly ripe yellow (or red) medium-size beefsteak tomatoes
¼ cup fresh grated Parmesan cheese
1 handful mixed baby greens
Sweet Shallot Vinaigrette (page 153)

In a medium bowl, combine the mushrooms with the olive oil, shallots, rosemary, and thyme; let sit for about 10 minutes.

Light a fire in a charcoal or gas grill. Using tongs, remove the mushrooms from the marinade and grill until slightly softened and browned, about 2 minutes on each side. Set them aside. (You can also complete this step ahead of time, refrigerate the mushrooms, and then bring them to room temperature when you're ready to stuff the tomatoes.)

Meanwhile, prepare the tomatoes so that you can use them to serve your salad in. Preheat the oven to 325°F. Using a sharp knife, slice the tops off the tomatoes either flat or in a zigzag pattern; you need them later so don't discard them. Using a melon baller or spoon, scoop out the insides. (You may want to save the insides for a sauce or another salad.) Set aside. Place the tomatoes into a 1-inch baking pan (you may have to adjust the bottoms, cutting carefully and only slightly, if they can't sit upright) with their tops. Bake until the skins start to wrinkle, about 15 minutes.

When the tomatoes are finished, remove the tops and stuff with alternate layers of the mushroom mixture and the cheese. Place the tomatoes back into the oven (without the tops) just until the cheese starts to melt, about 5 minutes.

Top each tomato with a bit of the mixed baby greens and a drizzle of the vinaigrette. Cover with the tomato tops, and serve.

TRIO ROASTED PEPPERS

in a Basil, Garlic, Olive Tapenade on Bruschetta Toasts

{ SERVINGS: 4 }

This topping is one you will find many uses for. You can make it ahead of time (up to 3 days in advance) and then, just before you're ready to serve this tasty appetizer, bring it to room temperature and toast up your bread! The slight sweetness of the brioche topped with the flavors of the roasted peppers is great, but you could certainly use another type of bread—like Italian or French.

¾ cup roasted green, red, and yellow peppers (see page 150), finely diced
3 teaspoons finely chopped kalamata or niçoise olives
1 teaspoon Garlic Oil (page 151)
3 basil leaves, rolled and chopped into thin ribbons (chiffonade, see page 26)
3 pieces toasted brioche (or, if you like firm bread, use 7-grain bread.)

In a medium bowl, combine the roasted peppers, olives, garlic oil, and basil. Mix well to form a spread.

Evenly divide the topping and spread it on the toast. Cut the bread in half on the diagonal, arrange on a dish, and serve.

GRILLED PORTOBELLO MUSHROOMS

brushed with Mint Pesto

{ SERVINGS: 4 }

If you're a mushroom lover, perhaps you're already enamored with the earthy, rich flavors of portobellos. This recipe will give you a simple, tasty way to expand your grilled mushroom repertoire. A perfect side dish for any grilled meat, these hearty mushrooms could also be part of a wonderful vegetarian meal, served with a leafy green salad. And, once you make the mint pesto that goes with this dish, you may just find yourself dreaming up other ways to use it!

4 portobello mushrooms (domestic or imported)
½ cup olive oil, plus additional for grilling
Kosher salt and freshly ground black pepper
½ cup rolled and finely cut mint leaves (chiffonade—see page 26)
¼ cup white balsamic vinegar
Juice of **½** orange
1 small shallot, minced
1 teaspoon honey
¼ cup chopped pecans

Light a fire in a charcoal or gas grill. Brush the mushrooms on both sides with olive oil and season with salt and pepper. Grill on both sides until just cooked through (you'll notice a bit of shrinkage and some water underneath), about 10 minutes all together.

Meanwhile, in a small bowl, combine the mint, ½ cup olive oil, vinegar, orange juice, shallot, and honey. Whisk together. Stir in the pecans. Place the mushrooms stem-side down on a serving plate. Brush the pesto on top of the mushrooms and serve immediately.

GRILLED SWEET PLANTAINS,

Abuelita Style

{ SERVINGS: 4 }

People who know me know that I often say, "Less is more!" This sweet side dish, which I learned to make from my *abuelita*—grandma—back in Colombia, definitely illustrates this credo. In this case, we're cooking up sweet plantains, which are quite different from the plantains you use to make tostones! These are encased in what will become a crispy wrapper, and subsequently become caramelized and soft. They're a perfect side dish, not unlike a potato or rice. One of the reasons that I love this grilled plantain, aside from the nostalgia it brings, is that it complements any grilled dish or salad. I've served it along with my Grilled Shrimp with Watercress and Sweet Corn Vinaigrette salad (page 49)—and it worked beautifully.

2 almost-black (very ripe) plantains, in their skins

Light a fire in a charcoal or gas grill. Using a sharp knife, cut a single, lengthwise slit in each of the plantains.

Place the plantains on the grill, rotating them as needed, until the skins are crispy, they start to open, and the plantain feels soft—like butter, about 15 minutes. Remove the plantains from the heat, cut them in the middle (widthwise), and place them on serving plates. Open the skin alongside the original slits and serve with a spoon for easy scooping. (Of course, you can also scoop out the plantains and place them in a serving dish—but it's much more fun to eat them straight from the skin!)

LESS IS MORE!

TOSTONES,
Ahogado Style

{ MAKES: 2 CUPS SOFRITO AND ABOUT 10 TO 14 TOSTONES }

Tostones—twice fried and smashed green plantains—are as ubiquitous in many parts of the Caribbean as French fries are in the United States. (The first time I was in Pereira, Colombia, I remember stopping by a roadside stand that was making the largest, flattest, and crispest tostones I have ever enjoyed!) The potato-like plantains, due to their rich, starchy flavor, are a great match for a fresh sofrito generously poured on top (hence the name, *ahogado*, which literally means "drowned"). Best served right out of the pan, tostones are perfect barbecue treats! Serve them as a snack, a side dish, or to accompany an ice-cold beer—or perhaps Strawberry Lemonade (page 127) or a Pomegranate Martini (page 136).

½ yellow onion, finely diced
1 teaspoon minced garlic
2 beefsteak tomatoes, finely diced
1 cup chicken stock
1 bay leaf
Kosher salt and freshly ground black pepper
1 tablespoon chopped cilantro leaves
2 to 3 large unripe (green or barely yellow) plantains
½ inch of canola oil

First, start the sofrito. Combine the onion, garlic, tomatoes, and chicken stock in a medium saucepan over medium-high heat. Add the bay leaf and season with salt and pepper. Bring to a simmer and then continue cooking on low heat until the tomato and onion have softened, about 10 minutes. Stir in the cilantro and remove from the heat.

Meanwhile, prepare the plantains. Green plantains can be very hard to peel. Soak them in warm water for about 15 minutes. Then cut a slit lengthwise down the plantain and open the skin by peeling it back (or use a knife to peel the skin). Slice the plantains crosswise into 1-inch-thick pieces. In a 12-inch, several-inch-deep nonstick skillet, heat the oil over moderate heat until the oil is just hot enough to sizzle when a plantain piece is added. Fry the plantains in batches, without crowding, until tender and just golden, 2 to 3 minutes on each side. With tongs, transfer the plantains to paper towels to drain.

Remove the skillet from the heat and reserve the oil. With the bottom of a heavy saucepan or a wide solid metal spatula, flatten the plantains until they're about a quarter of an inch thick and about 3 inches wide in diameter.

Heat the reserved oil over moderate heat until hot but not smoking. Fry the flattened plantains in batches, without crowding, until golden, about 3 minutes. Using tongs, transfer the twice-fried plantains to paper towels to drain and season with salt. Top with the sofrito sauce and serve immediately.

BOILED YUCA

with Cilantro Garlic Mojo

{ SERVINGS: 4 }

Lucky for me—and my family—I get to leave chilly New York and head to Miami from time to time. And it's there, at Boater's Grill in No Name Harbor Restaurant in Key Biscayne, where I've had some of the best boiled yuca. This is my interpretation of that dish, which I make for my family and friends as an easy barbecue side dish. You can use fresh yuca, but so many folks complain to me that they don't want to deal with the hefty bark. I recommend that they use frozen yuca, which is available in many large markets around the country.

1 teaspoon butter
1 teaspoon minced garlic
½ plum tomato, finely diced
Juice of **2** limes
1 pinch cilantro
1 twenty-four-ounce bag frozen yuca (available in large supermarkets and Latin American markets), preferably Costa Rican
Kosher salt and freshly ground black pepper

In a small saucepan over medium heat, melt the butter. Add the garlic and sauté until fragrant, about 2 minutes. Add the tomato and lime juice and remove from the heat. Add the cilantro and set aside.

Place the yuca in a large pot and pour enough water to cover by 2 inches; you'll need to check the liquid now and then and keep it at this level. Bring to a boil, reduce the heat, and simmer uncovered for about 35 minutes or until tender. Remove the yuca from the stock with a slotted spoon and let drain. Using your fingers, remove the string from the cores of the yuca and cut into ¼-inch-wide sticks. Place the yuca on a platter, season with salt and pepper, and pour the mojo on top. Serve immediately.

GRILLED PINEAPPLE COCONUT RICE

{ MAKES: ABOUT 2½ CUPS }

As my writer, Arlen, will tell you, there seem to be limitless variations of coconut rice in one of my favorite cities: Cartagena, Colombia. Born of the influence of African, indigenous, and European flavors, this rice is found in restaurants and homes throughout that coastal region. (My favorite interpretation, by the way, can be found in Cartagena's famous restaurant, La Vitrola!) In my version, I grill the pineapple in order to bring out its sweet flavors, which are balanced by the milk-infused rice. Serve this dish with any grilled meat or chicken—like Grilled Skirt Steak with Rosemary and Thyme Chimichurri Sauce (page 83) or the Grilled Sirloin with Chipotle-Mango Barbecue Sauce (page 81).

½ pineapple, peeled, cored, and cut lengthwise into 10-inch-wide slices for grilling
1 teaspoon grated fresh ginger
1 teaspoon cream of coconut
4¼ cups coconut milk
Juice of **½** lime
5 fresh mint leaves, stacked, rolled, and cut into fine shreds
2 cups long grain rice, rinsed

Light a fire in a charcoal or gas grill. Grill the pineapple until browned on both sides, 3 to 5 minutes. When cool enough to handle, cut the pineapple slices into ¼-inch dice. In a large bowl, combine the pineapple, ginger, cream of coconut, and ¼ cup of the coconut milk. Stir in the lime juice and mint leaves. Set aside.

Meanwhile, prepare the rice. In a medium heavy pan with a tight-fitting lid, heat the 4 remaining cups of coconut milk to just about a boil. Pour in the rice, stir, and bring to a boil again. Cover and reduce the heat to very low. Let cook, undisturbed (though you may need to add just a bit more liquid—water—if the rice looks as if it's getting too dry), until the liquid is absorbed and the rice is cooked through and tender, about 20 minutes. Add the grilled pineapple mixture and let sit for about 10 minutes before serving.

GRILLED MAINE LOBSTER SKEWERS

with a Mango-Basil Relish

{ SERVINGS: 4 }

Summer is the time when I especially like creating different combinations for my family—and customers; this is an example of a dish that I have made many times both at home and at work. The flavors of sweet, juicy mango and almost minty basil leaves combine to create a refreshing—and colorful—relish. This East-meets-West side dish (or appetizer!) is perfect for a summer's day. Serve with Mango Sangría (page 131).

1½ red onions (1 tablespoon minced; the rest cut into chunks for threading on the skewers)
¼ cup olive oil
1 tablespoon chopped basil leaves (about 10 leaves)
2 mangoes (1 cup diced; the rest cut into 1-inch chunks for threading on the skewers)
2 tablespoons white balsamic vinegar
1 teaspoon curry paste
4 lobster tails (about 1¼ pounds of meat) blanched for 4 minutes, removed from the shell, and cut into 1-inch chunks
1 Japanese cucumber, peeled and cut into 1-inch chunks for threading on the skewers
1 handful frisée lettuce

In a medium bowl, combine the minced red onion, olive oil, chopped basil, and diced mango. Stir in the balsamic vinegar and curry paste. Using a potato masher or fork, smash the contents together, leaving the mango still in larger chunks. Set aside. (There will be about ¼ cup of relish; it will keep for up to 3 days.)

Soak 8 bamboo skewers in water for about 30 minutes before grilling so they won't burn.

Light a fire in a charcoal or gas grill. Thread a skewer starting with a chunk of the lobster, then mango, then red onion, then cucumber, and finish with another lobster chunk. Repeat for the other 7 skewers. Place them on the grill and cook, just for about 2 minutes, to finish cooking the lobster and heat through.

Using about 2 tablespoons of the relish, coat each of the skewers. Spread the frisée lettuce on one or two serving plates and place the skewers on top. Serve immediately.

MEAT & POULTRY

(CARNE Y POLLO)

{Chapter 3}

The main attraction of any barbecue is the *plato principal*—the main dish. When I'm cooking at home, after a week of cooking for hundreds of people in the restaurants, I yearn to satisfy my own food cravings. My family—like me—enjoys meat, so you'll see a wide selection including beef, lamb, pork, and chicken. As a family, we also like variety (I've trained them well!) in the meats as well as the marinades, glazes, and toppings. Other criteria for my at-home cooking? Keep it simple—but delicious, of course. As always, I encourage you to try these recipes, use these guidelines as a base, and then—when you feel like it—create some of your own interpretations!

OPPOSITE: *Grilled Sirloin with Chipotle-Mango Barbecue Sauce*

Now we're getting serious

MEAT

(CARNE)

GRILLED CHORIZO

(Colombian Sausage) with Ají Rojo

{ SERVINGS: 4 }

It's not just because of my heritage that I love Colombian sausage! Maybe it's the combination of garlic, green onions, cumin, and cilantro. These spices manage to find their way into many of my dishes, but that's understandable: their flavors bring back great childhood memories for me *and* they're delicious. Here I've combined their flavors with my interpretation of a traditional Colombian salsa: *ají rojo*. The sauce—which is great on top of everything from chips to yuca—is easy to prepare, and it's great to keep on hand for other grilled meat dishes.

½ red onion, finely diced
Juice of **1** lime
1 red tomato, diced
½ cup olive oil
¼ cup white balsamic vinegar
½ habañero chile, peeled, seeded, and finely diced
1 teaspoon chopped chives
1 teaspoon chopped cilantro leaves
4 Colombian chorizo links

In a large bowl, combine the onion, lime juice, tomato, olive oil, and balsamic vinegar. Add the chile, chives, and cilantro and stir well. Let the mixture sit for at least 15 minutes. (This can be done several hours ahead of time; keep it in the refrigerator and bring it to room temperature just before serving.)

Light a fire in a charcoal or gas grill. Cook the sausages, turning every couple of minutes, until cooked through, about 10 minutes. (The grilling time will vary depending on the thickness of the sausages.) Remove the sausages from the grill and place them on a chopping board. Slice each sausage into rounds (on a slight angle) and place on a platter, or onto four plates. Top with the *ají rojo* and serve.

GRILLED PORK CHOPS

with Passion Fruit–Jalapeño Barbecue Sauce

{ SERVINGS: 4 }

Even before I worked with Mark Miller—the "founder" of Southwestern cuisine—I was smitten by barbecue sauces. Mark's passion for his cooking inspired me to make sauces using the flavors I knew and loved. (This philosophy is what drives all of my creations—both inside and outside the restaurants!) In this combination, the sweet-tartness of passion fruit makes it a natural for a barbecue sauce, and the slight bite of the smoky jalapeño also adds balance and depth. And remember, a barbecue sauce is versatile; here I'm using it to top off the fabulous flavors of grilled pork, but you can certainly use it with other meats—like grilled chicken. Also, once you make it, I'm sure you'll find other ways to have this sauce be a frequent visitor to your fiestas!

1 tablespoon canola oil
½ teaspoon minced garlic
½ red onion, diced
1 cup fresh orange juice
½ cup passion fruit nectar
2 roasted jalapeños (see page 150), deveined, seeded, and minced
½ cup ketchup
1 tablespoon fresh mint leaves, cut into thin ribbons
Four 1¼-inch-thick pork rib chops (12 ounces each with bone)
Kosher salt and freshly ground black pepper
Olive oil for brushing

Heat the oil in a medium sauté pan over medium-high heat. Add the garlic and red onion and cook until softened, about 3 minutes. Pour in the orange juice and passion fruit nectar, add the jalapeños, and let simmer until slightly reduced, between 8 and 10 minutes. Remove from the heat. Stir in the ketchup and mint. Transfer the sauce to a bowl; cool to room temperature, about 1 hour, and use immediately or cover and chill until ready to use. (This sauce can be made up to 3 days ahead. Bring to room temperature before serving.)

Light a fire in a charcoal or gas grill. Sprinkle the pork chops with salt and pepper. Brush them with olive oil. Grill the chops until just cooked through, about 8 minutes per side. Transfer them to a plate and let rest for about 10 minutes. Serve with the barbecue sauce. (I like to leave it on the side, but you can also put a bit on top of each chop.)

GRILLED LAMB CHOPS

with a Pomegranate-Citrus Glaze

{ SERVINGS: 4 }

Pomegranate was not a flavor I grew up with. In fact, I never even tried it until I spent some time working in San Francisco, for Bradley Ogden in Compton Place. I remember first seeing it cut in half, seeing the fantastic contrast of the off-white inside pulp, in which the bright wine-colored seeds are found. The flavors of the seeds are deep—sometimes sour and tangy and other times sweet. You can start this dish off with a Pomegranate Martini (page 136) and serve it with Grilled Caesar Salad (page 47) or, for a different combination of flavors, the Grilled Asparagus Spears with Wisconsin Blue Cheese Vinaigrette (page 56) or the Grilled Pineapple Coconut Rice (page 67).

24 ounces 100 percent pomegranate juice
Juice of **1** orange
2 shallots, minced
Zest of **1** lemon
6 quarter-inch-thick lemongrass slices (If unavailable, lemon or lime juice can be used—though the flavor will be different, of course.)
16 baby lamb chops, Frenched (ask your butcher to do it), fat trimmed to ⅛ inch
Kosher salt and freshly ground black pepper

In a medium saucepan over medium-high heat, combine the pomegranate and orange juices. Stir in the shallots, lemon zest, and lemongrass slices. Simmer until reduced by half, about 10 minutes. Set aside.

Light a fire in a charcoal or gas grill. Season the lamb with salt and pepper. Grill the lamb chops to desired doneness (5 minutes over medium heat, per side, for medium-rare). Let rest 1 to 2 minutes. Serve topped with the pomegranate glaze.

GRILLED LAMB CHOPS

with a Niçoise Chimichurri Sauce

{ SERVINGS: 4 }

The flavors in this dish bring me back to when I spent a year working for legendary French chef Michel Guérard, in Eugénie les Bains, France. Though, of course, chimichurri is Argentine pesto, the ingredients in this dish—primarily the combination of the olives and the lamb—are certainly French inspired! This chimichurri could work with any grilled meat—and even chicken, vegetables, or your favorite crusty bread! Serve this with Hombre Pobre (Poor Man's Salad) (page 45) or Grilled Caesar Salad (page 47).

Vegetable oil
8 to 12 lamb chops
Kosher salt and freshly ground black pepper
1 cup pitted niçoise olives
½ cup sun-dried tomatoes, coarsely chopped
1 teaspoon Garlic Oil (page 151)
½ cup olive oil
¼ cup white balsamic vinegar
½ cup chopped cilantro leaves
1 small shallot, minced
2 teaspoons honey
Juice of **½** orange

Light a fire in a charcoal or gas grill. Lightly oil and season both sides of the chops with salt and pepper. Cook the lamb chops to desired doneness (about 5 minutes over medium heat, per side, for medium-rare). Let rest 1 to 2 minutes.

Meanwhile, in a blender or food processor, combine the olives, tomatoes, garlic oil, olive oil, and balsamic vinegar. Add the cilantro, shallot, honey, and orange juice. Purée. Brush the chimichurri on the lamb chops prior to serving. Spoon additional chimichurri into a small dish for adding to the chops or spreading on bread.

GRILLED LAMB CHOPS

with Sun-dried Tomato Chimichurri

{ SERVINGS: 4 }

Ever since I started making sun-dried tomato chimichurri, I've found all kinds of ways to use it: as a dipping sauce, a marinade, and even a topping, as I'm sharing with you here. As far as the meat for this recipe, at Greenwich Tavern, I've been using New Zealand lamb chops. They are somewhat smaller than our domestic counterparts, but both are fine here. If you are using domestic lamb chops, two per person should be plenty.

8 to 12 lamb chops
Olive oil
Kosher salt and freshly ground black pepper
1 handful arugula or mesclun lettuce
1 tablespoon Sun-dried Tomato Chimichurri (page 153)
1 tablespoon grated goat cheese

Light a fire in a charcoal or gas grill. Lightly brush the chops with a bit of oil and season both sides of the chops with salt and pepper. Cook the lamb chops to desired doneness (about 5 minutes over medium heat, per side, for medium-rare). Let rest 1 to 2 minutes.

Sprinkle the arugula on a large platter. Decoratively arrange the lamb chops on top. Lightly spoon the chimichurri on the arugula and sprinkle the goat cheese on top of the chops. Serve immediately.

GRILLED SIRLOIN

with Chipotle-Mango Barbecue Sauce

{ SERVINGS: 4 }

As my father always said, "There's no reason to reinvent the wheel." However, I always say there's plenty of room for adding on! Many times I am inspired to build on something I've enjoyed in a restaurant; this is the case with Peter Luger's fabulous barbecue sauce. Here I'm infusing a bit of another couple of my favorite barbecue flavors (chipotle and mango) to build on the base that I love to use as a topping for grilled sirloin. (Once you try this sauce, you'll probably want to use it on fish, other meats, and even vegetables.) I suggest serving this dish with Grilled Caesar Salad (page 47) and Mango Sangría (page 131).

4 tablespoons mango pulp (or reduced mango nectar)
½ cup Peter Luger's Steak Sauce (available through the restaurant Web site—PeterLuger.com—or through Amazon.com)
2 teaspoons Chipotle Purée (page 145)
1½ pounds boneless sirloin steak, 1¼ inches thick
1 teaspoon olive oil
Kosher salt and freshly ground black pepper

Light a fire in a charcoal or gas grill. In a medium saucepan over medium heat, combine the mango pulp, steak sauce, and chipotle purée. Heat through, stirring constantly.

Meanwhile, brush both sides of the steak with the oil, followed by the salt and pepper. Grill until medium-rare and slightly charred around the edges, 4 to 5 minutes per side. Remove the steak from the grill and let it rest for 3 to 5 minutes. Slice the steak ½-inch thick against the grain. Drizzle the chipotle-mango sauce over each serving. Serve immediately.

GRILLED SKIRT STEAK

with Basil-Garlic Olive Oil

{ SERVINGS: 4 }

The first time I enjoyed a *churrasco*—skirt steak—wasn't in my native Colombia, but at the home of my sister's Argentine friends in Rye, New York! It was the beginning of a wonderful relationship (between skirt steaks and me)! The nice thing about the tasty skirt steak is that it offers cooks/diners a beautiful backdrop for a myriad of flavors. In this case, the light basil-garlic oil offers a perfect balance. Serve with crusty bread to sop up the additional oil.

1 bunch basil, blanched (dipped quickly—about 10 seconds—into boiling water and then into an ice bath) and stemmed
1 garlic clove, roasted (see page 151)
1 cup Garlic Oil (page 151)
2 pounds skirt steak
Kosher salt and freshly ground black pepper

In a food processor or blender, combine the basil leaves and roasted garlic. Slowly add the oil and process until well blended. Set aside.

Light a fire in a charcoal or gas grill. Season the steak generously with salt and pepper. Grill the skirt steak over high heat, about 3 to 4 minutes on each side for medium-rare. Remove the steak from the grill and let it rest for about 5 minutes. Slice the steak thinly against the grain, and drizzle with the basil-garlic oil. (You can keep some on the side for guests to add as desired.) Serve immediately.

GRILLED SKIRT STEAK

with Rosemary and Thyme Chimichurri Sauce

{ SERVINGS: 4 }

Grilled skirt steak is enhanced by this France-meets-Argentina chimichurri; the pungent, piney nuances of the rosemary and thyme balance beautifully with the taste of the flavorful meat. Serve with the Hombre Pobre Salad (page 45), the Grilled Caesar Salad (page 47), or any green leafy salad and crusty bread to sop up the additional oil.

½ habañero chile, peeled, seeded, and minced
1½ teaspoons chopped fresh thyme leaves
1½ teaspoons chopped fresh rosemary leaves
Juice of **2** limes
¼ cup olive oil
⅛ cup white balsamic vinegar
Kosher salt and freshly ground black pepper
2 pounds skirt steak

Light a fire in a charcoal or gas grill. In a blender, combine the habañero, herbs, lime juice, olive oil, and vinegar and process until well blended. Season with salt and pepper.

Season the steak generously with additional salt and pepper. Grill the skirt steak over high heat, about 3 to 4 minutes on each side for medium-rare. Remove the steak from the grill and let it rest for about 5 minutes. Slice the steak thinly against the grain and drizzle with the rosemary and thyme chimichurri. (You can keep some on the side for guests to add as desired.) Serve immediately.

GRILLED PALOMINO BURGER
with Manchego Cheese and Avocado

{ SERVINGS: 4 }

I was born in Colombia and raised in Queens, so this burger is an illustration of my cultural connections. Burgers, in my book, are great any time—whether it's in the middle of summer or in the cooler fall days, in between kicking back and watching the New York Jets! I like putting avocado or guacamole (my Latin American roots!) on top as much as I like adding a bit of melted Manchego cheese (the Spanish in me!). My kids, however, generally prefer their burgers with white Cheddar cheese. Regardless of how you top them, serve these burgers with your favorite cold beer or with Blueberry and Raspberry Margaritas (page 140).

Kosher salt
Vegetable oil
2 pounds ground sirloin beef, formed into four 8-ounce, ½-inch-thick patties
8 slices (or as desired) of Manchego cheese or white Cheddar cheese
4 brioche or your favorite rolls
1 ripe avocado, peeled and sliced, or **1 cup** Palomino's Guacamole (page 34)

Light a fire in a charcoal or gas grill. Spread a dash of the salt and a squirt of vegetable oil to both sides of each beef patty. Cook the burgers until medium-rare (or just below the desired degree of doneness), about 10 minutes on each side. Add the cheese to the burgers after you've flipped them the first time. Then place the rolls on the grill to toast. (They may take less time to toast than the burgers take to finish, so keep your eye on them!)

When the cheese starts to melt, remove the patties from the grill. Place the toasted buns on individual plates, top with the burger, and add the avocado slices before serving.

(POLLO)

ARROZ CON POLLO,

Palomino Style

{ SERVINGS: 4 TO 6 }

Arroz con pollo is the quintessential Latin American rice-and-chicken dish that is interpreted differently from culture to culture—and even from family to family. The wonderful thing about it is that it's flexible, simple, and comforting. Reminiscent of paella, this recipe is my family's interpretation. I love the one-pot-dinner feature of this dish! Start with one of my salads or ceviches and use this as your main entrée. Add some wonderful crusty bread and a salad on the side, and you're set. And another nice thing about arroz con pollo is that if you have any left over, it's great the next day, too!

3 tablespoons olive oil
2 teaspoons minced garlic
1 red onion, finely diced
1 yellow bell pepper, julienned
1 red bell pepper, julienned, plus **1 cup** roasted red bell peppers (see page 150), julienned
3 Colombian sausages (chorizo) or Italian-style sausages, sliced into ½-inch chunks on a slight angle
1 free-range chicken, 2½ to 3 pounds, cut into 8 serving pieces, or 2½ to 3 pounds of chicken thighs or breasts, bone-in, with skin on, rinsed and patted dry (You can also remove the skin so it's less fatty.)
1 pinch saffron
1 pinch cumin
7 sprigs thyme leaves
2 bay leaves
¼ cup (about 5) green olives
1 teaspoon capers
6 cups chicken stock
3 cups long-grain rice
Kosher salt and freshly ground black pepper

Pour the olive oil into a large stock pot, set over medium-high heat. When the oil is fragrant (but not smoking), add the garlic, onion, bell peppers, sausages, and chicken, skin-side down. Let the chicken brown on both sides, about 15 minutes, stirring the other ingredients as needed. Stir in the saffron, cumin, thyme, and bay leaves, along with the olives and capers, and cook until warmed through, another few minutes. Add the chicken stock and bring to a boil. Stir in the rice and bring to a boil again. Cover and simmer until the rice is cooked and fluffy, about 45 minutes. Stir to mix well, season with salt and pepper, and serve.

GRILLED CHICKEN AND WHITE CHEESE ROMAINE LETTUCE CHIPOTLE TACOS

{ SERVINGS: 4 }

Sundays are my days with my kids. And as much as I love to cook, I am not always into logging lots of kitchen time when I'm out of the restaurants! This is a quick and tasty kid (and adult) crowd-pleaser. Ideally you would make the hard-shell tacos on your own, but if you're busy—as most of us are—you can buy a box of 'em. (Just make sure you buy them from a store that has a lot of turnover of stock so you'll know they are not stale.) You can vary the toppings according to what's available, but these are my kids' favorites.

¼ teaspoon paprika
¼ teaspoon ground cumin
¼ teaspoon garlic powder
⅓ cup vegetable oil
4 boneless free-range chicken breasts, sliced into strips
½ teaspoon (or more, according to taste) Chipotle Purée (page 145)
½ cup sour cream
10 taco shells
2 plum tomatoes, diced
¾ cup chopped romaine lettuce
4 tablespoons grated white Cheddar cheese

Combine the paprika, cumin, and garlic powder. Add the oil and mix well. In a bowl (or plastic bag), combine the chicken with the spices and oil mixture. Make sure the chicken is well coated. Cover and refrigerate for at least 15 minutes or up to 3 days.

Combine the chipotle purée with the sour cream.

Light a fire in a charcoal or gas grill. Grill the chicken, turning once, until cooked through, about 5 minutes all together.

Lay out the taco shells in a work space. Place one quarter of the chicken strips in each shell. Then add the tomatoes, lettuce, and white Cheddar. Top with dollops of chipotle sour cream and serve immediately.

GRILLED CHICKEN MINI BROCHETTES
with Avocado and a Mango-Honey-Mustard Glaze

{ MAKES: 8 SKEWERS }

Maybe it's the sweet-tartness of the honey-mustard glaze, but this dish has been a crowd-pleaser for kids and adults since I first created it one sunny summer afternoon! Perfect as an appetizer or a main dish, this can be served with a salad, along with Grilled Arepas with Farmer's Cheese (page 37) and Tortillas with Palomino's Guacamole (page 34). And to drink, Mango Lemonade (page 128) and/or Pineapple and Raspberry White Sangría (page 130) are nice choices.

1 cup mango purée
3 tablespoons honey
1 teaspoon Pommery mustard
1 pinch paprika
1 pinch cumin
2 teaspoons canola oil
4 boneless and skinless chicken breasts, cut into sixteen ¾-inch chunks
2 medium ripe avocados, peeled, pitted, and cut into 1-inch chunks (to have at least 16 chunks) [Note: If they're too mushy, they'll fall apart.]
2 medium red onions, cut into 1-inch chunks (so you have about 16 chunks)
Kosher salt and freshly ground black pepper
1 handful baby arugula or mesclun lettuce

Soak 8 six-inch bamboo skewers in water for about 30 minutes before grilling so they won't burn.

In a small saucepan, combine the mango purée, honey, and mustard and mix well. Cook over medium heat until reduced by half, about 10 minutes. Set aside.

In a large bowl, combine the paprika, cumin, and oil and mix well. Add the chicken chunks and stir to coat. Cover and refrigerate for about 10 minutes.

Thread the skewers in the order of chicken, avocado, onion, chicken, avocado, and finish with onion. After all the skewers have been threaded, lightly brush them with the glaze.

Light a fire in a charcoal or gas grill. Place the skewers on the grill, season with salt and pepper, and grill until cooked through, turning as needed, about 7 minutes.

Place the arugula on a serving platter. Arrange the chicken skewers on top. Drizzle additional glaze as desired. Serve immediately.

ROASTED MUSCOVY DUCK
in a Honey–Black Pepper–Pineapple Glaze

{ SERVINGS: 4 }

It wasn't until I was a 19-year-old living (and learning!) in France that I learned to incorporate the striking flavor of freshly ground black pepper. Here, in this pineapple glaze, I think it works very well with the duck—though really this simple and tasty glaze is easily adaptable for use alongside pretty much any grilled meat. I tend to go heavier on the pepper than most folks, but I leave that up to you.

12 ounces pineapple juice
½ cup honey
Juice of **2** limes
Juice of **1** orange
2 tablespoons white balsamic vinegar
Freshly ground black pepper
4 duck breast halves, boned
Kosher salt

In a medium saucepan over medium-high heat, combine the pineapple juice and honey. Cook, stirring from time to time, until the juice is reduced by half, about 10 minutes. Stir in the lime and orange juices and the balsamic vinegar and a pinch of pepper. Set aside.

Meanwhile, place the duck breasts on a clean work surface. Trim off any excess fat and skin around the breast. There should be just enough skin to cover the breast. Shave off any additional skin or sinew on the surface of the meat. Using a very sharp knife and being careful not to cut into the meat, score the skin of the duck breasts in a crisscross pattern. (This allows the fat to render during cooking, which will result in crispier skin.) Season both sides with salt and pepper.

Place a large sauté pan over high heat until very hot. Sear the breasts until some of the fat has melted and the skin is brown and crisp, about 7 minutes. Pour off the fat and discard. Turn the breasts and continue cooking for 5 or so minutes, or until the duck breasts are still pink in the center. When ready to serve, slice each breast, fan out on the plate, and drizzle the honey glaze on top.

**KEEP IT SIMPLE,
BUT DELICIOUS!**

SHELLFISH & SEAFOOD

(MARISCOS Y PESCADO)

{ Chapter 4 }

I think that a lot of people feel that seafood is very complicated to make—and subsequently shy away from preparing fish dishes at home. If that sounds like you, I'd like to try to convince you otherwise! Seafood dishes really don't take too much time to prepare, and excellent-quality seafood doesn't need too much embellishment; it really speaks for itself. Besides, the flavors and textures are clean, fresh, and elegant.

Even before I opened my first Pacífico restaurant—which boasts a primarily seafood menu—I'd been a big fan of shellfish and seafood. Now, two Pacíficos later, I'm still exploring the wonderful world of fruits from the sea. This chapter introduces you to some of my patrons' favorite dishes, as well as many of those that I like to cook in my own home. As always, serving accompaniments are suggested.

OPPOSITE: *Grilled Sea Scallops with a Cumin and Garlic Rub*

So good—so easy—it's ridiculous

SHELLFISH

(MARISCOS)

GRILLED EAST COAST OYSTERS

with Corn Jalapeño Salsita

{ SERVINGS: 3 }

I've been a big fan of the plump and succulent wonders of oysters for a long time—since even before I started frequenting one of my favorite raw bars: the one in the Blue Ribbon, in Tribeca. Something about the charm of this particular example of our sea's bounty has always intrigued me. These days I prefer local (like Cape Cod) over other types of oysters, but, still, I'm open! The accompanying salsita—which is tasty all by itself or even spread on a small salad of your favorite greens—offers a wonderful flavor and texture balance. I suggest making the accompanying sauce ahead of time so you can visit with your guests. Then just grill the oysters, plate them, and serve.

4 ears corn, shucked
Canola oil for grilling
2 plum tomatoes, sliced in half, lengthwise
1 red onion, sliced
Freshly ground black pepper
1 jalapeño pepper, roasted (see page 150), deveined, seeded, and diced
2 tablespoons olive oil
2 tablespoons white balsamic vinegar
Kosher salt
12 oysters, scrubbed

Light a fire in a charcoal or gas grill. Place the corn—without anything on it—on the grill grate. Grill the ears of corn, rotating the corn as needed to keep it from getting charred too much on one side, for about 7 minutes. (Don't overcook the corn, or it will become mushy!) Remove from the heat and let cool slightly. Remove the kernels from the cobs and set aside.

Meanwhile, squirt just a bit of canola oil on the tomato and onion slices. Sprinkle pepper on top. Place the onion slices on the grill. Add the tomatoes cut-side down on the hot grate and grill until both are nicely browned, 3 to 5 minutes. Turn the onion slices and tomatoes with tongs and continue grilling until the bottoms of the tomatoes (the rounded parts) are nicely browned and the onion becomes softer and fragrant, about 2 more minutes.

Dice the onion and tomatoes and place in a bowl. Add the corn kernels and the jalapeño. Pour in the olive oil and vinegar and stir to combine. Season with salt. This can be done up to one day ahead of time; just bring the salsita to room temperature prior to serving.

Place the oysters directly on the grates of the grill, close the cover, and cook until all of the oysters have opened, 4 to 5 minutes. Discard any oysters that have not opened on their own. Further open the ones that have started to open and top each one with 1 teaspoon of the corn and jalapeño salsita. Serve hot.

GRILLED SEA SCALLOPS
with a Cumin and Garlic Rub

{ SERVINGS: 4 }

Maybe it's my Italian heritage that has caused me to be so enamored with the flavors of braised garlic. *Mi abuelita*—my grandma—taught me well: braising brings out the best in garlic, whether it's for a pasta sauce, for a rub, or even just for a spread on crisp toasts (yes—and it does cure everything!). This is a super-simple recipe that you can put together in no time at all. I suggest serving your grilled sea scallops with Grilled Pineapple Coconut Rice (page 67) and ice-cold beer or a pitcher of Pineapple and Raspberry White Sangría (page 130).

¼ cup olive oil
8 garlic cloves, cut into ¼-inch dice
1 teaspoon cumin
1 tablespoon cilantro
Juice of **¼** lime
12 large sea scallops, side muscles trimmed, halved horizontally
Kosher salt and freshly ground black pepper

In a large heavy skillet, heat the olive oil over medium-low heat. Add the garlic and lower the heat to the lowest possible setting. Cook, covered, for about 5 minutes. Uncover and continue cooking over the lowest possible heat until the garlic is barely colored to pale brown and tender, about 8 minutes. Stir it frequently and be sure not to let the garlic brown too much, or it will be bitter. Add the cumin, cilantro, and lime juice and mix well. Scrape the mixture into a blender and pulse just until well blended. Set aside.

Thread the scallops onto 4 metal skewers (3 to a skewer) and coat them with the braised garlic mixture. Sprinkle with salt and pepper.

Light a fire in a charcoal or gas grill. Grill until the scallops are just opaque in the center, occasionally brushing with more garlic, about 3 minutes per side. Serve immediately.

GRILLED JUMBO SHRIMP
and Sun-dried Tomato Chimichurri

{ SERVINGS: 6 }

This is one of my favorite summertime home-barbecue treats. I like it because the flavors are terrific (and it's quite popular with my wife and kids!) but also because it's so simple. I make the chimichurri ahead of time (honestly I always have some in my fridge—and I sell it by the jar in the restaurants!) and then just buy my jumbo shrimp when the spirit moves me . . . which is just about every weekend during the steamy Sundays of July and August. Serve your shrimp atop a bed of frisée lettuce; the contrast between the crispy shrimp and the smooth, clean lettuce is great. I like to serve this dish with grilled sourdough bread.

12 ounces (about 1½ cups) sun-dried tomatoes, soaked in hot water for 20 minutes
2 tablespoons roasted garlic (see page 151)
¼ cup white balsamic vinegar
Juice of **1** lime
1 cup olive oil
Kosher salt and freshly ground black pepper
18 uncooked jumbo shrimp, cleaned and deveined with tails intact
Frisée lettuce

In a blender or food processor, combine the sun-dried tomatoes, garlic, vinegar, lime juice, and oil. Process until well blended. Season with salt and pepper. Let sit for about 20 minutes (or, cover and refrigerate for up to 3 days and return to room temperature before serving).

Take about ½ cup of the sun-dried tomato chimichurri and rub it on the shrimp. Let the shrimp marinate, covered in the refrigerator, for at least an hour.

Light a fire in a charcoal or gas grill. Remove the shrimp from the marinade, brushing off the chunks of chimichurri (so it doesn't burn). Thread the shrimp on 6 metal skewers (3 to a skewer). Grill the shrimp until cooked through, about 2½ minutes per side.

Prepare six small plates or martini glasses with a small bed of frisée lettuce, place the shrimp on top, and serve. You can also serve the shrimp on a platter with extra sun-dried tomato chimichurri for dipping.

GRILLED ECUADORIAN SHRIMP

with a Cilantro and Garlic Marinade

{ SERVINGS: 2 }

First I should confess: I really don't think that being in a country's airport counts as being in that country. However, on my way down to Lima, Peru, I did stop in Quito, Ecuador, where I tasted one of the most amazing airport snacks I've ever had—Ecuadorian shrimp ceviche. I had never tried Ecuadorian shrimp before, and I was immediately smitten! Now this isn't that ceviche, but the freshness of those flavors has inspired many creations, including this one. For more than two servings, simply multiply accordingly.

6 large shrimp, peeled (with tails on) and deveined
1 teaspoon minced garlic
Leaves from **2** sprigs thyme
1 tablespoon chopped cilantro leaves
1 pinch cumin
Kosher salt
1 tablespoon olive oil
Hombre Pobre (Poor Man's Salad) (page 45) or a salad of your choice

Place the shrimp in a bowl and add the garlic, thyme, cilantro, and cumin. Season with salt, stir in the olive oil, and mix so that the shrimp is well coated. Let sit for about 15 minutes.

Light a fire in a charcoal or gas grill. Place the shrimp on the grill and grill until cooked through, about 2½ minutes per side.

Prepare a serving plate with the salad. Place the shrimp on top and serve.

GRILLED LOBSTER TAILS
with Paprika-Garlic Oil

{ SERVINGS: 4 }

Lobster tails are always tasty (no need for dipping butter—though I do love that, too!), and very simple to make. Florida, Caribbean, or rock lobster tails are the best to grill, but you could also use Maine lobster tails. I suggest combining them with my Grilled Caesar Salad and making the meal family style.

4 lobster tails (8 to 10 ounces each), fresh or frozen
4 tablespoons Garlic Oil (page 151)
½ teaspoon paprika
Grilled Caesar Salad (page 47) or a salad of your choice

Fill a stock pot about three-quarters of the way up with water. Boil the tails until the shells are red and the meat is opaque (frozen, about 12 minutes; fresh, about 8) and firm. (Be careful not to overcook them, or they'll get rubbery.)

Light a fire in a charcoal or gas grill. When the tails are cool enough to handle, split them in half lengthwise. In a bowl, combine the garlic oil and paprika and whisk together. Using a brush, cover the lobster meat with the oil. Place the tails on the grill and cook, just for about a minute, to heat through.

Cut the lobster tails in half again (this time horizontally!) so that they're easy to pick up. Prepare a serving plate with the salad. Place the lobster tails on top and serve.

“

FISH ON THE GRILL IS
CLEAN, FRESH, AND ELEGANT.

”

Wonderfully Speedy and Delicious

(PESCADO)

GRILLED YELLOWFIN TUNA,
Yucatan Style

{ SERVINGS: 6 }

Many moons ago, when I worked in Jams—where Jonathan Waxman created the California cuisine–inspired Jams restaurant menu—I remember first combining a minimal number of ingredients to create maximum flavor. This dish—which is also reminiscent of citrus-infused fish dishes I enjoyed in Mexico's Yucatan Peninsula—is simple, clean, and delicious. Serve this grilled tuna with the Grilled Caesar Salad (page 47) and glasses of Mango Sangría (page 131).

1 tablespoon canola oil, plus additional oil for brushing
6 five-ounce tuna steaks
Juice of **4** oranges
Juice of **2** limes
2 tablespoons grated ginger
1 teaspoon soy sauce
1 teaspoon honey
1 tablespoon chopped cilantro leaves

Light a fire in a charcoal or gas grill. Lightly oil both sides of each of the steaks (just so they're well coated), and grill to desired doneness, about 3 minutes per side for medium-rare. Meanwhile, combine the citrus juices, ginger, soy sauce, and honey. Stir in the 1 tablespoon oil and blend well. Add the cilantro and mix again.

Set up six serving plates. Remove the tuna from the grill. Slice each tuna steak and arrange the slices on each plate. Drizzle the sauce over each sliced steak and serve immediately.

GRILLED WASHINGTON SALMON STEAK
with a Soy Panela Glaze

{ SERVINGS: 4 }

Panela is the Colombian sweetener I grew up with. It looks like a roll-size loaf of hard-packed brown sugar and has a lovely, caramelized and syrupy rich sweet flavor. *Panela*—called *chancaca* in Peru and *piloncillo* in parts of Central America and the Caribbean—is used to make a variety of drinks, desserts, and breads. Here, I'm combining it with soy sauce to create a sweet-salty balance that, along with the lemongrass and ginger, adds a *toque*, or touch, of Asian influence to the rich salmon steak flavor. Serve this fish with Grilled Pineapple Coconut Rice (page 67) and your favorite Cabernet—or Mango Sangría (page 131).

2 cups water
½ cup soy sauce
Juice of **2** oranges
4 tablespoons *panela* (available in Latin markets) or dark brown sugar
½ stick lemongrass, chopped
4 thin slices ginger
Olive oil
4 eight-ounce organic wild-salmon steaks

In a medium saucepan, combine the water, soy sauce, orange juice, *panela*, lemongrass, and ginger. Bring to a boil. Continue cooking until the sauce thickens and becomes more of a glaze (about 20 minutes). Strain and set aside.

Light a fire in a charcoal or gas grill. Lightly oil both sides of each steak (just so they're lightly coated) and grill to desired doneness, about 4 minutes per side for medium-rare. Remove from the grill and, using a brush, coat each side of the salmon with the glaze before serving.

GRILLED HAWAIIAN TUNA

in a Soy and Citrus Marinade

{ SERVINGS: 4 }

There's such beauty in simple dishes like this one. The clean flavors of the pineapple, orange, and lime juices are a perfect match with this quickly marinated tuna. Start this dinner with Grilled Pineapple Mojitos (page 133) and serve the fish with your favorite leafy green salad and a side of Grilled Pineapple Coconut Rice (page 67) for a Hawaiian luau with a Latin touch!

½ cup pineapple juice
Juice of **2** oranges
Juice of **2** limes
2 green onions
2 tablespoons soy sauce
4 five-ounce albacore tuna steaks (about 1-inch thick)

In a medium bowl, combine the fruit juices, green onions, and soy sauce and stir just to combine. Set the tuna steaks in a deep glass dish and pour the soy-citrus marinade on top. Cover and refrigerate for about 10 minutes.

Light a fire in a charcoal or gas grill. Remove the steaks from the marinade (but save the marinade!) and grill the tuna steaks to the desired doneness, about 4 minutes per side for medium-rare. Pour the remaining marinade into a saucepan and reduce by half, about 10 minutes. Strain. Slice the tuna and drizzle the sauce on top. Serve immediately.

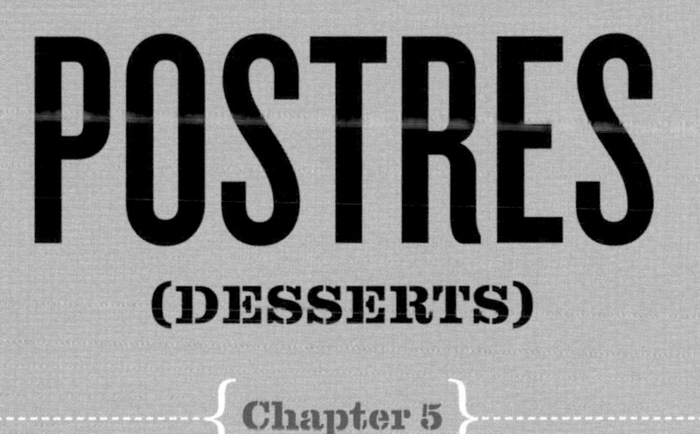

Anybody who knows me knows that I've got a sweet tooth. My menus in all the restaurants reflect an assortment of treats that I've created based on my heritage, experiences, and, of course, what I enjoy! Desserts have always made me happy. When my sister, brother, and I were kids, my dad would take us to the Siete de Agosto market in Bogotá and treat us to not only the dazzling show of all the vendors hawking their luscious wares but also fabulous fruit desserts. Those scenes come back to me every time I make treats like grilled plantains with guava and melted mozzarella—and see my own son's eyes widen with delight! Here, I introduce readers to a carefully honed selection of my personal favorites—which I hope you'll enjoy making for yourself, your family, and your friends.

OPPOSITE: *Semisweet Chocolate and Coffee Brioche Bread Pudding*

Leave 'em with a sweet taste in their mouths

POSTRES

(DESSERTS)

GRILLED SWEET PLANTAINS

Topped with Guava and Melted Mozzarella

{ **SERVINGS: 6** }

These are my Colombian-style s'mores! And just like former campers may grow misty at the mere mention of that campfire treat, when I make this at one of my restaurants, the eyes of my Colombian employees swell with tears because this *postre,* or dessert, is so near and dear to their hearts! Little by little, this Colombian Napoleon is winning new fans; they enjoy the combination of the sweet guava and plantain, balanced by smooth melted mozzarella. This dessert is easy to prepare ahead of time and makes for a very colorful finish to any meal.

3 very ripe plantains, unpeeled (They should be black.)
8 ounces mozzarella cheese, cut into ⅛-inch-thick slices
8 ounces guava paste (available in both Latin American markets and large grocery stores), cut into ⅛-inch-thick slices
Vanilla ice cream (optional)

Light a fire in a charcoal or gas grill. Without cutting all the way through, slice the still-in-their-skin plantains lengthwise. (You want to be able to fill them, so they need to be attached in the back.)

You're going to stuff the plantains with three layers: start with one of mozzarella, then another of guava in the middle, and top with another of mozzarella. Wrap each plantain tightly in foil and place all of them on the grill.

Cook the plaintains until the mozzarella and guava have melted, about 15 minutes. Then unwrap each one, cut them in half crosswise, and immediately place the plantains on serving plates. Top with vanilla ice cream, if desired, and serve.

CHURROS

with Dulce de Leche, Mora, or Chocolate Sauce

{ **SERVINGS: 4 TO 6** }

This Spanish-born deep fried dough treat—like many others—has made its way north from Latin America all the way to the United States. Churros are perfect party fare, first and foremost because who can resist fried dough (?!) and, second, because they can be served with a variety of tasty sauces, as presented here (though my kids like them plain, with just a bit of cocoa and sugar sprinkled on top). To make the characteristic log-shaped churros, I suggest spooning the mixture into a pastry bag with a ½-inch star tip (the kind used to decorate cakes).

2 cups water
3 tablespoons unsalted butter
3 tablespoons granulated sugar, plus **½ cup** for rolling
2½ cups all-purpose flour
1 pinch salt
2 eggs, at room temperature

Canola oil for deep frying
Dulce de Leche Sauce (page 147)
Mora Sauce (page 149)
Chocolate Sauce (page 146)

In a medium saucepan over medium heat, combine the water, butter, and the 3 tablespoons sugar. Bring to a boil and cook, stirring constantly, until the butter is completely melted and the sugar is dissolved. Remove from the heat. Add the flour quickly, all at once. Using a sturdy whisk, stir until smooth. Add the salt. Let rest for 2 minutes. Then add the eggs, one at a time, and stir/mix well.

Cover a sheet pan with parchment paper. Spoon the batter into a pastry bag. Squeeze five or six 3-inch lengths of the mixture onto the baking sheet, using a knife to slice off each length as it emerges from the nozzle. Let rest for about 10 minutes.

Heat 4 inches of oil in a deep, heavy pot to 375°F, or in a deep-fryer according to the manufacturer's instructions, until a piece of dried bread floats and turns golden in the oil after 1 minute. Cook the churros, in batches as needed, until golden. Quickly drain on paper towels and roll in the ½ cup of sugar while still warm. Serve immediately, with the sauces as desired.

COCONUT FLAN
with Guava Sauce

{ **SERVINGS: 6** }

This tropical-flavored flan is the perfect sweet finale for a fabulous barbecue—and one of my family's favorites. Make your flan the day before the soirée so you don't have to worry about it the day of. Also, you can always double this recipe to have more to send home with your guests or to serve during the week. And keep in mind that though here I'm suggesting a simple guava fruit topping, you can always try mango, passion fruit, or pineapple—or a combination of all of the above!

1 cup water
¼ cup granulated white sugar
3 eggs, plus **3** egg yolks
1⅓ cups whole milk
1⅔ cups sweetened condensed milk
1 tablespoon cream of coconut
1 teaspoon vanilla extract
2 tablespoons Guava Sauce (page 148)
1 tablespoon toasted coconut, for garnish

Combine the water and sugar in a medium saucepan over medium heat. As soon as the mixture begins to bubble, stir it and reduce the heat to low. Cook, stirring frequently, until the mixture turns medium brown, about 15 minutes. Pour the caramel into six 4-ounce ramekins.

Preheat the oven to 350°F. In a large mixing bowl, beat the eggs and yolks with a wire whisk until foamy. Beat in the whole milk, sweetened condensed milk, cream of coconut, and vanilla. Pour the mixture over the top of the caramel in the ramekins. Create a water bath by filling a roasting pan halfway with hot water. Put the ramekins in the roasting pan and cover with foil. Bake the flan-filled ramekins until the centers are soft but firm, about 25 minutes. Remove the cups from the bath, let them cool to room temperature, and then cover and refrigerate for at least 4 hours and up to 24 hours.

Just before serving, run a knife around the edge of each ramekin and flip the flan onto a plate. (If you're having trouble getting it out, place the ramekin in a dish of hot water for about 10 minutes to loosen.) Drizzle the guava sauce and sprinkle the coconut flakes on top just before serving.

SEMISWEET CHOCOLATE AND COFFEE BRIOCHE BREAD PUDDING

{ SERVINGS: ABOUT 8 }

This pudding is to desserts what the Hombre Pobre (Poor Man's Salad) (page 45) is to salads; it's an excellent way to use leftover bread. However, there's nothing wrong with buying bread specifically to make this pudding! This dessert, as Arlen discovered when she first made it, is just dreamy; if you're a chocolate lover, then this is absolutely for you. The comforting texture and mocha flavor are perfect on those chillier fall days. It's also a great dessert for entertaining because you put it together the night before and bake it an hour before dessert time. Enjoy with coffee, dulce de leche, vanilla, or your favorite ice cream and/or fresh whipped cream.

2 cups heavy cream
6 ounces semisweet chocolate, grated, or ½ pound of semisweet chocolate chips
1 tablespoon vanilla extract
5 eggs
1 cup granulated sugar
¼ cup coffee liqueur
½ loaf brioche, about 8 ounces, or 4 rolls, torn or sliced into bite-size pieces (or challah bread, crust removed and sliced into ¼-inch pieces)

In a medium saucepan over medium heat, combine the cream and chocolate and cook, stirring frequently, until the chocolate is melted and the mixture is smooth. Stir in the vanilla. Let cool slightly.

In a medium bowl, combine the eggs with the sugar and whisk together. Add the chocolate mixture and the coffee liqueur. Continue whisking until the sugar is dissolved.

Butter an 8-inch baking pan. (You can also use individual ramekins, but the cooking time will be shorter, about 25 minutes.) Add the brioche and ladle the chocolate mixture over the brioche. Let stand, covered loosely, at room temperature for at least 1 hour. (You also have the option of covering and chilling the bread mixture overnight.)

Preheat the oven to 325°F. Put the baking pan in a larger pan so you can make a bath; add enough hot water to the larger pan to reach halfway up the sides of the baking pan. Bake the pudding in the middle of the oven until a skewer inserted in the center comes out clean, about 60 minutes. (But begin checking doneness after 50 minutes.) Serve the pudding warm.

COCONUT TRES LECHES CAKE

{ **SERVINGS: 15** }

I don't think I've ever been to a family celebration that didn't serve *pastel de tres leches*! And just like I hear my Italian friends boasting about their mother's and grandmother's lasagna ("Mine makes the BEST!"), you'll hear many Latinos boasting about their mom's version of this sweet and tasty sponge cake. So titled for its inclusion of three different kinds of milk, this dessert is super-easy to make—and if you have any left over, it's great warmed and served with *café con leche* in the morning. Serve with ice cream, whipped cream, or fruit sauce— or all three.

½ cup unsalted butter
¾ cup sugar
6 large eggs
1 teaspoon vanilla extract
1½ cups all-purpose flour
1½ teaspoons baking powder
1 cup milk
1 fourteen-ounce can sweetened condensed milk
1 twelve-ounce can evaporated milk
1 tablespoon cream of coconut
2 tablespoons shredded coconut, lightly toasted

Preheat the oven to 325°F. Butter an 8-by-12-inch glass baking dish. In a medium bowl, beat the butter and sugar at medium speed with an electric mixer until fluffy. Add the eggs and vanilla. Combine the flour and baking powder and gradually add it to the butter mixture. Mix until blended; be careful not to overmix the batter. Pour the batter into the prepared dish and bake until the cake is puffed and golden and the edges pull away from the sides of the pan, about 30 minutes.

Combine the three milks and cream of coconut in a blender and mix until well blended. Poke holes all over the cake with a bamboo stick, wooden pick, or skewer. Spoon 3 of the 4 cups of the milk mixture over the cake (you can reserve the remaining cup and give people the option of pouring some over their serving). Cover the cake and chill in the refrigerator for at least 30 minutes, or overnight. Sprinkle the toasted coconut on top just before serving.

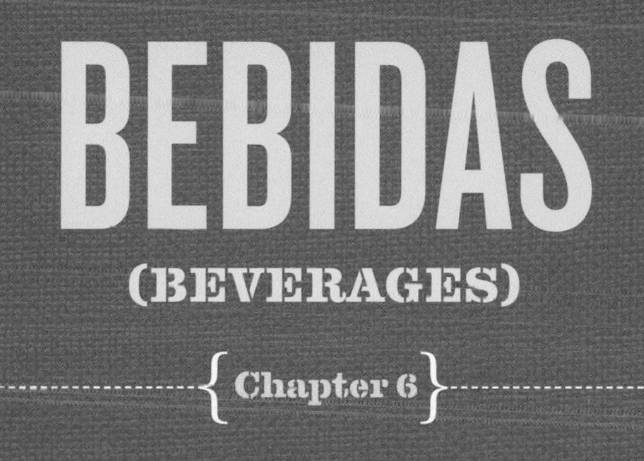

BEBIDAS

(BEVERAGES)

{ Chapter 6 }

The job of a Latin flavor–infused *trago*—or cocktail—is not to distract from the food but to enhance it. This chapter contains a great selection of my favorite juices and cocktails. Exotic and exciting, yet not too difficult to prepare, these are ideally suited for people looking to expand their own—and their families' and guests'—beverage horizons.

In many of my recipes, I've suggested accompanying cocktails. However, I encourage you to start thinking about what drinks would marry well with which dishes. The challenge should be fun! And who knows? In the process you might just start coming up with your own creative variations!

OPPOSITE: *Mango Sangría*

Not just for the thirsty

(BEVERAGES)

STRAWBERRY LEMONADE

{ SERVINGS: 1 }

This drink is perfect for kids and adults of all ages. And you can multiply the quantity and keep a pitcher on hand (be sure to adjust the sugar accordingly!) or make it on command!

1 lemon, quartered
6 teaspoons sugar
4 strawberries, hulled and quartered
4 ounces water
4 ounces Sour Mix (page 152)
1 cup ice, plus more for serving
4 teaspoons mango purée

In a large bar shaker, combine the lemon, sugar, and 3 of the strawberries. Using a pestle, muddle them until the strawberries become a purée. Add the water, sour mix, the 1 cup ice, and mango purée. Cover and shake vigorously.

Fill a bar glass with ice. Strain the lemonade into the glass. Garnish with the remaining strawberry and serve.

MANGO LEMONADE

{ SERVINGS: 1 }

The sweet flavors of mango work so well with the tartness of lemon. This is a perfect barbecue drink—for both kids and grown-ups! (Grown-ups, by the way, can make this drink "more grown-up" by mixing it with a touch of rum!)

4 lemon wedges
2½ teaspoons sugar
3 teaspoons Simple Syrup (page 152)
1 ounce Sour Mix (page 152)
4 teaspoons mango purée
1 cup ice, plus more for serving
Water

In a large bar shaker, combine the lemon wedges, sugar, simple syrup, and sour mix. Using a pestle, muddle them together. Add the mango purée, the 1 cup ice, and water to fill up the shaker. Cover and shake.

Fill a bar glass with ice. Strain the mixture into the glass and serve.

BLUEBERRY-PISCO SOUR

Even before I traveled to Peru, I enjoyed sipping pisco sours, that country's national cocktail. I've also had the opportunity to introduce many people, through my restaurants, to the great flavors of this drink, which is a perfect start to any summertime barbecue or fiesta. One day in Sonora, when we were playing around with different variations of the drink, we came up with one using the fruit that means summer to me: the blueberry. I'm sure you'll enjoy this colorful and tasty cocktail no matter what you're celebrating!

2 tablespoons mashed fresh blueberries
3 tablespoons superfine sugar
3 tablespoons freshly squeezed lime juice
4 ounces pisco (Peruvian grape brandy)
1 large egg white
1 cup crushed ice
Angostura bitters

Chill two heavy tumblers or martini glasses in the freezer. In a bar glass, combine the fresh blueberries with the sugar and lime juice. Using a pestle, muddle them until well blended. Scrape into a blender. Add the pisco, egg white, and ice and process until foamy.

Pour the mixture into the chilled glasses and add a few drops of bitters on top. Serve immediately.

PINEAPPLE AND RASPBERRY WHITE SANGRÍA

{ SERVINGS: 1 }

This is one of my wife Martha's favorites. She loves the combination of flavors, so I make it for her whenever she puts in a request! (And I'm sure you know that as much as I want to keep my customers happy, my family's always number one!) This is great with an afternoon barbecue or a late morning brunch.

4 ounces white wine
1 cup ice
¾ teaspoons Simple Syrup (page 152), or to taste
¾ ounce Triple Sec
1 ounce raspberry purée
1 ounce brandy
2 ounces pineapple juice
1 splash fresh orange juice
3 teaspoons chopped fruit (oranges, Granny Smith apples, etc.)

In a large (10-ounce) wine glass, combine the wine and ice. Stir in the syrup, Triple Sec, raspberry purée, brandy, and fruit juices. Add the fruit and stir. Serve immediately.

MANGO SANGRÍA

{ SERVINGS: 2 }

This simple sangría is perfect when you are looking for a cocktail on the lighter side. I suggest you keep chopped fruit on hand with a bit of fresh lemon juice. (That's what we do in the restaurant!) That way you can stir these up as soon as your guests walk through the door. Here, I've given you the recipe for two drinks (so you'll divide these ingredients into the glasses accordingly), but you can multiply this—and even make a pitcher of sangría!

16 ounces white wine, such as sauvignon blanc
2 cups ice
3 teaspoons (or to taste) Simple Syrup (page 152)
2 ounces Cointreau
3 tablespoons mango purée
4 tablespoons chopped fruit (oranges, Granny Smith apples, etc.)
4 ounces lemon-lime soda

In two large (10-ounce) wine glasses, pour the wine and ice. Stir in the simple syrup, Cointreau, and mango purée. Add the fruit and stir. Top off each glass with the lemon-lime soda, stir once, and serve immediately.

GRILLED PINEAPPLE MOJITO

{ SERVINGS: 1 }

Grilling the pineapple enhances its natural sweetness; the caramelized fruit complements this mint and lime cocktail. For more than one serving, simply multiply accordingly.

3 half-inch chunks of grilled pineapple (see page 148)
8 mint leaves
3 lime wedges
1½ cups ice
2½ ounces white or pineapple rum (the latter adds more pineapple flavor)
½ ounce Sour Mix (page 152)
1 splash club soda

In a large bar shaker, combine the pineapple, mint, and lime. Using a pestle, muddle them just until you've broken up the pineapple a bit and released the juice from the lime. Add the ice, rum, and sour mix. Cover and shake vigorously.

Pour the mixture into a bar glass, top off with the club soda, and serve.

KIWI MOJITO

{ SERVINGS: 1 }

Since its arrival in New York not too long ago, this Cuban-born cocktail has won over scores of fans. This interpretation is gorgeous—and refreshing. It offers a nice counterbalance to any of the heftier meat dishes but can also beautifully complement salads—like the Grilled Shrimp with Watercress and Sweet Corn Vinaigrette (page 49).

1 kiwi, quartered
1½ teaspoons sugar (or to taste)
7 mint leaves
1 lime, quartered
1½ cups ice
2 ounces white rum
½ ounce Sour Mix (page 152)
1 splash club soda

In a large bar shaker, combine the kiwi, sugar, mint, and lime. Using a pestle, muddle them just until you've released the juice from the lime. Add the ice, rum, and sour mix. Cover and shake vigorously.

Pour the mixture into a bar glass, top off with club soda, and serve.

MANGO AND SAKE MARTINI

{ SERVINGS: 1 }

I'm still learning about sake—Japanese rice wine. Though I like it on its own, I also enjoy combining it, as I've done in this case, with the tropical flavors of mango.

1 cup ice
4 ounces sake
1½ ounces mango purée, plus **1** mango slice for garnish
Juice of **1** lime wedge
½ teaspoon Simple Syrup (page 152)

In a bar shaker, combine the ice, sake, mango purée, lime juice, and simple syrup. Cover and shake vigorously.

Strain the mixture into a chilled martini glass, garnish with the mango slice, and serve immediately.

POMEGRANATE MARTINI

{ SERVINGS: 1 }

This is such a gorgeous drink! It's elegant—and powerful. And, well, you know that pomegranate juice is good for you!

1 lemon twist
2 cups ice
4 ounces 100 percent pomegranate juice
2 ounces vodka (or lemon vodka)

Rub the rim of a chilled martini glass with the lemon twist and let it drop into the center of the glass.

In a bar shaker, combine the ice, pomegranate juice, and vodka. Cover and shake vigorously. Strain into the prepared glass and serve immediately.

DULCE DE LECHE MARTINI

{ SERVINGS: 1 }

This Latino-style white Russian is a beautiful after-barbecue drink . . . perfect for when the night starts to cool off. Then again, you could—if you have a sweet tooth as I do—start your evening with this one!

2 cups of ice
1 tablespoon Dulce de Leche (page 146)
1½ ounces vanilla vodka
Toasted coconut flakes for garnish

In a bar shaker, combine the ice, dulce de leche, and vodka. Cover and shake vigorously.

Strain the mixture into a chilled martini glass, garnish with the toasted coconut, and serve immediately.

STRAWBERRY AND CUCUMBER COSMOPOLITAN

{ SERVINGS: 1 }

This is truly one of the most refreshing cocktails I've ever had! There's something so cooling about cucumber—and even if you're not a big cucumber fan, this drink may just move you to the other side. On a steamy day, this is perfect with one of the ceviches—or just about anything.

2 strawberries
1 teaspoon sugar
6 very thin cucumber slices (with skin)
2 teaspoons Sour Mix (page 152)
1½ cups ice
1½ ounces lime vodka
½ ounce Triple Sec

In a large bar shaker, combine the strawberries, sugar, 4 cucumber slices, and the sour mix. Using a pestle, muddle them until the strawberries become a purée. Fill the bar shaker with ice. Add the vodka and Triple Sec. Cover and shake vigorously.

Strain the mixture into a chilled martini glass, garnish with the 2 remaining cucumber slices, and serve.

WATERMELON AND KIWI COSMOPOLITAN

{ SERVINGS: 1 }

This drink is so festive and refreshing. You can multiply the ingredients according to the numbers of guests you have, make up a pitcher, and keep it in the fridge until you're ready to pour!

1 cup ice
1 kiwi, quartered, plus
1 slice for garnish
1½ teaspoons sugar
(or to taste)
2 ounces watermelon purée
1½ ounces lemon vodka
1 ounce Triple Sec

In a large bar shaker, combine the ice, kiwi, sugar, watermelon purée, vodka, and Triple Sec. Cover and shake vigorously.

Strain the mixture into a chilled martini glass, garnish with the kiwi slice, and serve.

BLUEBERRY AND RASPBERRY MARGARITA

{ SERVINGS: 1 }

Because there's such a wonderful selection of frozen fruit these days, you can make this drink any time of year. (I suggest putting your fresh raspberries and blueberries in the freezer for one of those winter days when you crave a taste of the tropics!) The flavors—and colors—of this margarita are so festive!

4 fresh raspberries
4 fresh blueberries
½ teaspoon sugar
2 cups ice
1½ ounces white tequila
2 ounces Triple Sec
½ ounce fresh lime juice
¾ ounce Sour Mix (page 152)

In a large bar shaker, combine 3 of the raspberries, 3 of the blueberries, and the sugar. Using a pestle, muddle them until well blended. Add the ice, tequila, Triple Sec, lime juice, and sour mix. Cover and shake vigorously.

Pour the mixture into a bar glass, garnish with the remaining berries, and serve.

POMEGRANATE AND RASPBERRY MARGARITA

{ SERVINGS: 1 }

I call this one my fall margarita! It's a deep wine red color, and it looks picture-perfect with a lime wedge garnish. Refreshing yet hearty, this drink goes really well with my burger (page 85)—or any of the grilled meat dishes.

8 fresh raspberries, plus additional raspberries for garnish
1 ounce pomegranate juice
2 cups ice
1½ ounces white tequila
1 ounce Triple Sec
½ ounce Rose's lime juice
½ ounce Sour Mix (page 152)
1 lime wedge for garnish

In a large bar shaker, combine the raspberries, pomegranate juice, ice, tequila, and Triple Sec. Add the lime juice and sour mix, cover, and shake vigorously.

Pour the mixture into a bar glass, garnish with the lime, and serve.

BASICS

(RECETAS BÁSICAS)

Chapter 7

There are certain must-have items that you'll find in both my restaurant and my home kitchens—like my roasted garlic and my chipotle purée. I'm sure that once you start incorporating these "basics," as I've suggested, you'll discover even more ways to weave them into your recipe repertoire.

CHICKEN STOCK

These days, there are wonderful organic chicken stocks that you can find on supermarket shelves, but I'm still of the school of "homemade is best!" Because chicken stock adds such flavor and depth to a variety of soups, stocks, and more, I find it to be a fundamental ingredient.

1 small free-range chicken (about 3½ pounds), quartered
10 cups cold water
1 teaspoon kosher salt
1 large stalk celery with leaves, coarsely chopped
2 carrots, peeled and coarsely chopped
1 onion, coarsely chopped
1 bay leaf
1 bunch cilantro or parsley, stemmed and coarsely chopped
Cloves from **1** small head garlic, peeled

Rinse the chicken well and trim off all excess fat. Put it in a large stockpot and add the water. Add the salt and bring to a boil. Skim off any fat or scum that rises to the surface. Add the remaining ingredients and reduce the heat to low. Simmer until the chicken is fork-tender, about 2 hours, skimming occasionally as necessary. Add water as needed to keep the chicken covered.

Pour the stock through a fine-mesh strainer into another pot or large bowl, pressing on the solids with the back of a large spoon to release the liquid. Spoon off the fat that rises to the top. You can make the stock even clearer by straining it through paper towels. Let cool to room temperature. Transfer to airtight containers and refrigerate overnight. Store in the refrigerator for up to 3 days or freeze for up to 3 months.

Makes: About 6 cups

CHIPOTLE PURÉE AND CHIPOTLE TARTAR SAUCE

This little ingredient—the chipotle chile—can liven up so many dishes, from sandwiches to salsas and much, much more! Chipotle chiles are smoked jalapeños; they are typically packed in adobo, which is a sauce made of tomato purée, onion, garlic, oil, vinegar, salt, bay leaves, and oregano. You'll find many uses for this purée. In fact, you'd never catch me without it—or the can of chipotles! To make my tartar sauce, purée the *chipotles en adobo* without the oil (as indicated) and combine it with mayonnaise and other ingredients as directed.

Chipotle Purée

1 thirteen-and-a-half-ounce can of *chipotles en adobo* (found in most large supermarkets and Latin American markets)
¼ cup vegetable oil

Empty the can of *chipotles en adobo* into a blender or food processor. Pour in the oil and blend until smooth. Cover and store in the refrigerator for up to 6 months.

Makes: About 1¾ cups

Chipotle Tartar Sauce

½ cup mayonnaise
1 tablespoon drained and chopped capers
1 tablespoon finely chopped gherkin or dill pickle
1 tablespoon fresh lime juice
1 tablespoon chipotle purée (blended without the oil)
Kosher salt
½ cup vegetable oil

Combine all the ingredients in a medium bowl. Adjust the seasoning, cover, and refrigerate until ready to use. This will keep for up to 5 days.

Makes: About ¾ cup

CHOCOLATE SAUCE

Though I am suggesting that you use this to drizzle atop your churros (page 117), you'll soon discover that this sauce is great spooned over pancakes—for a super Sunday brunch—or over coffee or vanilla or your favorite ice cream! For kids or a non-alcohol-imbibing crowd, simply eliminate the coffee liqueur.

3 ounces semisweet chocolate
1½ teaspoons granulated sugar
⅓ cup heavy cream
1½ tablespoons coffee liqueur, such as Kahlúa

In a small saucepan or the top part of a double boiler, combine the chocolate, sugar, and cream. Cook over moderate heat, stirring constantly, until smooth. Turn off the heat and stir in the coffee liqueur at the last moment. Keep warm until ready to serve.

Makes: About ¾ cup

DULCE DE LECHE (CARAMELIZED MILK) AND DULCE DE LECHE SAUCE

Dulce de leche is one of those sweets that you can constantly find uses for. And, to be quite honest, you can—as my kids do—enjoy it by the spoonful, too! Here are two recipes: one is the recipe my *abuelita*—my grandmother—used, and the other is a less labor-intensive method.

Grandma's Dulce de Leche

4 cups whole milk
2 cups sugar
¼ teaspoon baking soda
2 pinches ground cinnamon

In a large saucepan, combine all the ingredients. Cook over medium heat, without stirring, for 15 to 20 minutes. Reduce the heat to low and cook for 25 to 30 minutes, stirring constantly with a wooden spoon. When the mixture thickens so much that you can see the bottom of the pan as you stir, remove from the heat. Let cool completely. Cover and store in the refrigerator for up to 2 weeks.

Makes: About 2 cups

Easy Dulce de Leche

1 fourteen-ounce can
sweetened condensed milk

Put the unopened can of sweetened condensed milk in a stockpot and add cold water to cover by 2 inches. Bring the water to a boil and cook for 1 hour and 45 minutes. Check the water often to make sure it is always covering the can. Also, do not let it cook for more than 2 hours; not only will you overcook the dulce de leche, but you will also run the risk of exploding the can (which, I am happy to report, has never happened in my family, though we have been making dulce de leche for many, many years). Using tongs, occasionally turn the can over to stir the milk.

Remove the can from the water and let cool completely before opening. Transfer the caramelized milk to an airtight container and store in the refrigerator for up to 2 weeks.

Makes: About 1¾ cups

Dulce de Leche Sauce

3 tablespoons dulce de leche
½ cup heavy cream

In a small saucepan over low heat, combine the dulce de leche and cream. Cook, stirring constantly, until smooth and slightly thickened, about 1 minute.

Makes: About ½ cup

GRILLED PINEAPPLE

Grilling this sweet, tropical fruit certainly enhances its flavor. Whether it's to put on rice, top fish, or serve atop pancakes (my kids' favorite!), grilled pineapple is something that, once you try, you'll make over and over again. Though I'm suggesting you cut the pineapple lengthwise, you can cut the pineapple into rounds and grill it that way.

1 pineapple, peeled, cored, and cut lengthwise into 10-inch-wide slices for grilling

Light a fire in a charcoal or gas grill. Grill the pineapple until browned on both sides, 3 to 5 minutes.

Makes: One grilled pineapple

GUAVA SAUCE

This simple sauce can be drizzled on top of coconut flan (page 118), churros (page 117), or your favorite ice cream!

¾ cup guava paste (available at Latin American markets and large supermarkets)
¼ cup water

In a small bowl, combine the guava paste and water and mix until blended. Put the sauce in a squeeze bottle. Use immediately or store in the refrigerator for up to 1 week.

Makes: About 1 cup

MORA SAUCE

The flavor of mora—or South American blackberries—is found in many of our desserts and sweets. This sauce is as great on coconut flan (page 118) as it is atop churros (page 117)—and much more!

1 cup puréed blackberries or raspberries (or a combination of the two!), strained
2 cups water
½ cup granulated sugar, or to taste

In a small saucepan or the top part of a double boiler, combine the berries, water, and sugar. Cook over medium heat, stirring constantly, until slightly thickened. Keep warm until ready to serve.

Makes: About 3 cups

MUSTARD VINAIGRETTE

This is another light vinaigrette for your collection. Though I recommend you try it with the Grilled Sea Scallops with Avocado and Apple Salad (page 51), I'm sure you'll find other salads that would be enhanced by this topping.

1 small shallot, minced
3 tablespoons Pommery mustard
¼ cup white balsamic vinegar
¼ cup vegetable oil
Kosher salt and freshly ground black pepper

Combine the shallot and mustard and mix well. Add the vinegar and mix well. Slowly whisk in the oil. Mix until well blended. Season with salt and pepper. Use immediately or keep refrigerated for up to 2 weeks.

Makes: 1 cup

PERUVIAN OLIVE, CILANTRO, AND THYME TAPENADE

Purple Peruvian olives are ideal for this tapenade, but kalamata are certainly a close second! This is great to keep on hand not only to use in recipes like Grilled Flour Tortillas with Goat Cheese, Peruvian Olives, and Roasted Red and Yellow Peppers (page 33) but also to simply spread on your favorite crusty bread!

½ cup white balsamic vinegar
½ cup olive oil
1 tablespoon mashed roasted garlic cloves (see page 151)
1 roasted red onion (see page 152), chopped
1 cup niçoise olives, pitted and finely diced
1 medium grilled (optional) tomato, finely diced
1 tablespoon minced fresh thyme
Kosher salt and freshly ground black pepper
1 cup fresh cilantro leaves, chopped

In a large bowl, whisk the vinegar, oil, and garlic together. Add the onion, olives, tomato, and thyme. Season with salt and pepper. Stir well, using your hand or a wooden spoon. Let sit for 20 minutes. Serve immediately or cover and refrigerate for up to 2 days. Return to room temperature and add cilantro just before serving.

Makes: About 2½ cups

ROASTED BELL PEPPERS AND CHILES

Nothing brings out the flavors in peppers and chiles like roasting them! I keep these handy in all kitchens to add color and flavor to everything from salads to soups—and grilled meats and fish. (I often make myself a roasted pepper sandwich—on a piece of my favorite Italian bread, with just a bit of oil and a piece of grilled chicken!)

To roast bell peppers and/or chiles:
Spike a whole bell pepper (or chile) with a long fork and hold it directly over a gas flame, place it on a grill over hot coals, or put it in a very hot cast-iron skillet. Turn the pepper until it is charred on all sides. Place in a plastic or paper bag and close the bag. Let sit for about 10 minutes or until cool to the touch. Pull out the stem and rub off the black skin. Cut the pepper in half and remove the seeds with your hands—don't use water or you will lose all those wonderful oils you worked so hard to get. Use right away or submerge in olive oil, cover tightly, and refrigerate for up to 3 days.

To roast peppers and/or chiles under a broiler:
Cut the bell peppers (or chiles) in half lengthwise. Core them and remove the seeds and ribs. Lay the peppers, skin-side up, on a baking sheet as close to the heat source of a preheated broiler as possible, and broil until the skins are charred. You may want to use kitchen gloves when dealing with hot chiles; if you have a small cut, those little seeds can burn.

ROASTED GARLIC AND GARLIC OIL

I have always loved the flavors of this fruit of the earth. And it's not just because my *abuelita* told me that garlic would cure me of all ailments nor because of my fear of vampires! Roasting garlic makes it even sweeter (and the fragrant aroma it exudes from the oven is just wonderful)! The oil is great on grilled shrimp, fish, lobster, sirloin, skirt steak—and more.

To roast single cloves of garlic in the oven:
Peel the garlic cloves, sprinkle them with a bit of kosher salt, and wrap them in foil. Place on a metal pan in a preheated 350°F oven for 12 to 15 minutes.

To roast a whole head of garlic:
Remove any loose skin from the garlic, wrap the garlic in foil, place on a baking sheet, and roast in a preheated 350°F oven for 45 minutes. The garlic will be roasted and tender. To remove, just squeeze the cloves out of the skin.

Garlic Oil

½ garlic clove, roasted, minced (It's like a paste, so you should cut and/or mash the garlic to break it into smaller pieces for mixing with the oil.)
½ cup olive oil
Juice of **1** small lime

Combine the three ingredients in a bowl and whisk until well blended. Keep for up to 3 weeks in the refrigerator.

Makes: About ¾ cup

ROASTED ONIONS

Both at home and in the restaurant, it seems like red onions are the first ones I reach for. I enjoy their somewhat sweeter flavor (though Vidalias are nice as well!), and they are supersimple to roast either on the grill or in the oven!

On the grill:
Remove each onion's dry outer skin. Lightly coat the onions with olive oil, add a bit of kosher salt, and place on the grill. Grill each side until the onions are slightly softened, about 3 minutes per side.

In the oven:
Remove each onion's dry outer skin. Lightly coat the onions with olive oil and sprinkle with kosher salt. Place the onions on a baking sheet. Roast in a preheated 350°F oven for about 45 minutes or until lightly browned.

SIMPLE SYRUP AND SOUR MIX

In the bars, we use sugar, simple syrup, and sour mix. Of course, you can buy sour mix, but it's pretty easy to make your own—and I promise it's worth the time investment!

Simple Syrup

1 cup water
1 cup sugar

In a medium saucepan, combine the water and sugar. Stir over medium heat until the sugar dissolves. Bring to a boil. Turn off the heat and let the syrup cool to room temperature before refrigerating. Store in the refrigerator for up to 1 week.

Makes: About 1 cup

Sour Mix

¾ cup water
¾ cup sugar
½ cup fresh lemon juice
½ cup fresh lime juice

In a medium saucepan, combine the water and sugar. Stir over medium heat until the sugar dissolves. Bring to a boil. Turn off the heat and let the syrup cool to room temperature. Add the lemon and lime juices and transfer to a container for the refrigerator. Store in the refrigerator for up to 1 week.

Makes: About 2 cups

SUN-DRIED TOMATO CHIMICHURRI

I started making this to serve with warm slices of fresh-baked bread at Pacífico, where it became an immediate hit! Many of my customers—who buy it by the jarful—tell me that they're still discovering ways to use it as a topping, dipping sauce and marinade.

½ cup dry-packed sun-dried tomatoes, soaked in hot water for 20 minutes and drained
½ cup white balsamic vinegar
5 cloves roasted garlic (see page 151)
1 cup olive oil
Kosher salt and freshly ground black pepper

In a blender or food processor, combine the tomatoes, vinegar, roasted garlic, and olive oil and process until well blended. Season with salt and pepper. Let sit for about 20 minutes and serve. Or cover and refrigerate for up to 3 days. Return to room temperature before serving.

Makes: About 1½ cups

SWEET SHALLOT VINAIGRETTE

This is a light and very easy vinaigrette. I recommend serving it with my Grilled Lamb with Gorgonzola and Goat Cheese and Frisée Lettuce salad (page 53)—or any salad on which you'd like to use a flavorful but light dressing.

½ cup minced shallots
1 tablespoon brown sugar
½ cup white wine vinegar
1 cup canola oil
Kosher salt and freshly ground black pepper

In a medium saucepan over medium heat, cook the shallots and sugar, stirring constantly, until the shallots start to soften and brown, about 3 minutes. Remove from the heat and combine the caramelized shallots, vinegar, and oil in a blender and mix until well blended. Season with salt and pepper. Chill for at least 1 hour before using. Use immediately or keep for up to 2 weeks.

Makes: About 2 cups

IT'S HARD TO USE A RECIPE IF YOU CAN'T

D

E

F

TABLE OF EQUIVALENTS

The exact equivalents in the following tables have been rounded for convenience.

Liquid/Dry Measurements

U.S.	Metric
¼ teaspoon	1.25 milliliters
½ teaspoon	2.5 milliliters
1 teaspoon	5 milliliters
1 tablespoon (3 teaspoons)	15 milliliters
1 fluid ounce (2 tablespoons)	30 milliliters
¼ cup	60 milliliters
⅓ cup	80 milliliters
½ cup	120 milliliters
1 cup	240 milliliters
1 pint (2 cups)	480 milliliters
1 quart (4 cups, 32 ounces)	960 milliliters
1 gallon (4 quarts)	3.84 liters
1 ounce (by weight)	28 grams
1 pound	448 grams
2.2 pounds	1 kilogram

Lengths

U.S.	Metric
⅛ inch	3 millimeters
¼ inch	6 millimeters
½ inch	12 millimeters
1 inch	2.5 centimeters

Oven Temperature

Fahrenheit	Celsius	Gas
250	120	½
275	140	1
300	150	2
325	160	3
350	180	4
375	190	5
400	200	6
425	220	7
450	230	8
475	240	9
500	260	10